BUS PRESERVATION AND RALLIES:
THE EARLY YEARS TO 1980

Front Cover: Seen at the third Bristol Rally and Avon Run held on 21 August 1977 is this superbly restored 1949 Albion Venturer CX19 with Metro-Cammell bodywork from the Cheltenham District fleet, complete with period advertisements. This was with the Coventry Bus Preservation Group at the time and is now kept at the BaMMOT Transport Museum at Wythall.

BUS PRESERVATION AND RALLIES:
THE EARLY YEARS TO 1980

Malcolm Batten

AN IMPRINT OF PEN & SWORD BOOKS LTD.
YORKSHIRE - PHILADELPHIA

First published in Great Britain in 2023 by
Pen and Sword Transport
An imprint of
Pen & Sword Books Ltd.
Yorkshire - Philadelphia

Copyright © Malcolm Batten, 2023

ISBN 978 1 39908 790 2

The right of Malcolm Batten to be identified as author of this work has been asserted by him in accordance with the Copyright, Designs and Patents Act 1988.

A CIP catalogue record for this book is available from the British Library.

All rights reserved. No part of this book may be reproduced or transmitted in any form or by any means, electronic or mechanical including photocopying, recording or by any information storage and retrieval system, without permission from the Publisher in writing.

Typeset in Palatino 10.5/14 by SJmagic DESIGN SERVICES, India.

Printed and bound in India by Replika Press Pvt. Ltd.

Pen & Sword Books Ltd incorporates the imprints of Pen & Sword Books Archaeology, Atlas, Aviation, Battleground, Discovery, Family History, History, Maritime, Military, Naval, Politics, Railways, Select, Transport, True Crime, Fiction, Frontline Books, Leo Cooper, Praetorian Press, Seaforth Publishing, Wharncliffe and White Owl.

For a complete list of Pen & Sword titles please contact

PEN & SWORD BOOKS LIMITED
47 Church Street, Barnsley, South Yorkshire, S70 2AS, England
E-mail: enquiries@pen-and-sword.co.uk
Website: www.pen-and-sword.co.uk

or

PEN AND SWORD BOOKS
1950 Lawrence Rd, Havertown, PA 19083, USA
E-mail: Uspen-and-sword@casematepublishers.com
Website: www.penandswordbooks.com

CONTENTS

Introduction	7
Timeline of Key Events	10
Museum of British Transport: 1961–1973	12
Still in Service: 1971–2	17
Imperial War Museum: 1970	19
Southampton University: 1971	20
HCVC London to Brighton Run: 2 May 1971	21
HCVC London to Brighton Run: 7 May 1972	25
Preserved London Buses Back in Use: 1972	28
HCVC London to Brighton Run: 1973	29
London Transport Collection, Syon Park: 1973	30
Southsea Rally: 10 June 1973	32
Weymouth Rally: 1 July 1973	34
Bus of Yesteryear Rally, Clapham Common: 15–16 September 1973	36
HCVC London to Brighton Run: 5 May 1974	38
Leicester Open Day: 28 July 1974	40
HCVC London to Brighton Run: 4 May 1975	43
Southsea Rally: 8 June 1975	45
Showbus Rally – Uxbridge: 28–9 June 1975	47
Rushmoor Arena Rally: 20 July 1975	50
Preservation Sites and Vehicles in the Mid 1970s	52
HCVC London to Brighton Run: 2 May 1976	56
London Transport Collection, Syon Park: 16 May 1976	58
Southend Rally: 6 June 1976	59
Southsea Rally: 13 June 1976	61
Showbus Rally – Uxbridge: 26–27 June 1976	63
National Tramway Museum, Crich: 28 August 1976	65
Victoria and Albert Museum: 1976	66
Cobham Bus Museum: 3 April 1977	67
HCVC London to Brighton Run: 1 May 1977	69
Southend Rally: 5 June 1977	71
Southsea Rally: 12 June 1977	72
Showbus Rally – Uxbridge: 25–26 June 1977	73

Bournemouth Open Day: 24 July 1977	75
Bristol Rally: 21 August 1977	76
Newcastle: Summer 1977	78
Cobham Bus Museum: 2 April 1978	79
HCVC London to Brighton Run: 7 May 1978	80
Enfield Pageant of Motoring: 28–29 May 1978	82
Southend Rally: 4 June 1978	83
Southsea Rally: 11 June 1978	85
Showbus Rally – Uxbridge: 24–25 June 1978	87
Weymouth Rally: 2 July 1978	88
Lancaster Rally: 16 July 1978	89
London Bus Rally, Brockwell Park: 22–23 July 1978	92
Newcastle: July 1978	93
Sandtoft Gathering: 30 July 1978	94
Bristol Rally: 20 August 1978	96
National Tramway Museum, Crich: 26–28 August 1978	97
London Transport Collection, Syon Park: 17 September 1978	98
Preservation Sites and Vehicles in the Late 1970s	100
HCVC London to Brighton Run: 6 May 1979	103
Southampton Rally: 6–7 May 1979	104
West Bromwich Rally: 13 May 1979	105
Southend Rally: 3 June 1979	107
Southsea Rally: 10 June 1979	108
Showbus Rally – Uxbridge: 23–24 June 1979	109
Weymouth Rally: 1 July 1979	111
London Bus Rally, Brockwell Park: 21–22 July 1979	113
Bristol Rally: 19 August 1979	114
150 Years of London Buses: 1979	115
Cobham Bus Museum: 13 April 1980	118
HCVC London to Brighton Run: 4 May 1980	120
East Anglia Transport Museum, Carlton Colville: 15 July 1980	122
Lincolnshire Vintage Vehicle Society	124
London Transport Museum, Covent Garden: 1980	126
Postscript	127
Bibliography	128

INTRODUCTION

The preservation of our transport heritage is something at which the British excel. True, most developed countries may have heritage railways and maybe a transport museum or two, but nowhere on the scale of the UK. The *Buses* magazine *Museum & Rally Guide 2020/21* lists forty museums in the United Kingdom plus one in the Republic of Ireland with collections of buses (and sometimes trams or trolleybuses) amongst their exhibits. The rally calendar section lists hundreds of events taking part every year. There is a monthly magazine *Bus & Coach Preservation* devoted to the subject and the PSV Circle publishes a regular updated guide to all known preserved buses, trolleybuses and trams, now estimated to be over 5,000.

This is all a fairly recent phenomenon, established since the 1950s. The story has been told of how the heritage railway movement was started by L.T.C. (Tom) Rolt when he proposed saving the Talyllyn Railway in 1950. He was also instrumental in pioneering the restoration of semi-derelict canals to navigable waterways. The Talyllyn was followed by the Ffestiniog Railway, then in 1960 the Bluebell Railway became the first standard gauge heritage line. Since then, the movement has mushroomed with at least one such line in almost every county. The 'Beeching Axe' created a range of potential lines; the decision by Dai Woodham not to cut up the steam locomotives at his Barry scrapyard (for commercial rather than sentimental reasons) created a source of ex-BR steam locos to run on these lines.

Also well known is the story of how a race for a wager between two traction engine owning farmers, Arthur Napper and Miles Chetwynd-Stapylton in 1950 led to the start of the traction engine rally scene. This soon became well established. In 2018, the fiftieth anniversary was celebrated by each of the Weeting rally, the Bedfordshire Steam Club rally, and the largest such event, the Great Dorset Steam Fair.

Not so well recorded is the history of bus preservation. Again, private preservation started in the 1950s. After some earlier attempts to save London buses which failed to raise the asking price, in 1956 AEC Regal T31 was bought by a group of six people including Ken Blacker, Michael Dryhurst and Prince Marshall for £45, to become the first privately preserved bus. This had become the last ex-London General bus still serving with London Transport, though by now relegated to training duties. The 1929 veteran had originally been fitted with a rear entrance and petrol engine. It was converted to front entrance and was given a diesel engine in 1950. After purchase it was then found that substantial restoration work would be needed to combat body rot. Undeterred, other enthusiasts followed suit and within twenty years many hundreds of buses had been purchased by private individuals and groups. Amongst these were a number of vehicles that had long ceased operational service and were rescued from dereliction or subsequent use as houses, chicken sheds etc. Many others were bought out of service, and there was also an increase in the preservation and operation of heritage vehicles by bus companies. Current national groups such as Stagecoach and Arriva have inherited some such vehicles in company acquisitions and have continued to retain significant vehicles as part of their heritage collections.

The 1950s was not the absolute beginning of preservation. On the railways, there had been some putting aside of locomotives from the early days by the Great Western and LNWR amongst others. The original Stephenson's *Rocket* had also been retained. Most such engines were not on public display. The only major transport organisation in the UK with a museum collection open to the public in the 1930s was the London & North Eastern Railway with its railway museum at York which was opened in 1928 following the 1925 Stockton & Darlington Railway centenary celebrations. Its nucleus was a collection of locomotives and artefacts retained by one of its constituents, the former North Eastern Railway. The GWR had *North Star* and *City of Truro* kept at Swindon but these were only accessible on visiting days to the works.

With buses and trams, a few far-sighted companies put aside some historic vehicles. The London General Omnibus Company and their successor London Transport were amongst these, and it is to their foresight that we owe the older part of the London Transport Museum collection. Again, these were not on display except on special occasions.

As the number of vehicles privately preserved began to increase, societies were established to bring together preservationists and arrange collective storage for the vehicles acquired. The Historic Commercial Vehicle Club (HCVC) was formed in 1958. When founded, it was a small group of enthusiasts with around a dozen vehicles between them but would soon grow. The Lincolnshire Vintage Vehicle Society followed in 1959, the Reading Transport Society in 1961 (forerunners of the British Trolleybus Society) and the London Bus Preservation Group in 1966.

Some early events were held by the HCVC and others from 1958 and into the 1960s, but the first regular annual event was the HCVC London-Brighton Run, first staged in 1962. The first HCVC Trans-Pennine Run started in 1969. These events were reported on in *Buses* magazine, itself published since 1949. But events in the 1960s were few and in the index to *Buses* magazine for 1969 the only events listed were the London-Brighton and Trans-Pennine Runs and a Rochdale Motorcade on June 15 to mark the end of municipals absorbed into the SELNEC Passenger Transport Executive with some preserved vehicles present. However, interest in old buses had grown to the extent that *Buses* magazine in August 1962 was advertising an Ian Allan 64-page publication titled *Veteran and Vintage Public Service Vehicles* by David Kaye with a photo of the HCVC London-Brighton Run on the cover which was being reprinted having sold 5,000 copies. *Buses* magazine was also featuring articles about vehicles being acquired for preservation. For instance, in December 1962 there was an article about the repatriation of a former Southdown 1936 Leyland Cub CUF 404 from Jersey for private preservation, a source for many pre-war vehicles at this time.

The 1960s also saw the establishment of museum sites. The Museum of British Transport opened in London in stages during 1963, and 1963 housed in a former tram depot. This would close in 1973 and be replaced in part by the London Transport Museum. In 1963, the HCVC had proposed that a Club Museum should be created, open to the public, and a site at Fleetwood was considered. However, this idea was later dropped. The East Anglia Transport Museum was started at Carlton Colville, near Lowestoft in 1965; and the Sandtoft Transport Centre Association was formed in 1968. Both of these would achieve working trolleybus wiring in the early 1970s. Already established was the Tramway Museum at Crich, who held their first Grand Transport Extravaganza in 1968.

Other than the HCVC-organised Runs, bus rallies would really take off in the 1970s, with several examples going on to become annual fixtures. One of the first of note was the Bus of Yesteryear Rally, held at Stratford-upon-Avon on 31 May 1970. This was organised by the London Bus Preservation Group. There were two classes and awards for former LT vehicles, pre-1945 (four entries) and post-1945 (eight entries). Provincial buses were divided into single and double-deck classes as well as by age, and another class which would become a feature for many later rallies was one for currently operating vehicles. A second Bus of Yesteryear Rally took place in central London on 23 May 1971 at the car park between County Hall and the Royal Festival Hall. This time there were 100 buses and coaches present including modern vehicles. Unfortunately, the weather was very wet. In 1972 it was held at the Somers Town goods yard in London (now the site of the British Library), and in 1973 on Clapham Common.

Probably the most significant new rally happened almost by accident when Brunel University's Omnibus Society agreed to provide some vintage buses as part of the University's Community Festival, 'Brunelzeebub' in January 1973. From this modest affair would come Showbus, the largest annual bus rally which will be celebrating fifty years in 2022, still organised by its founder Martin Isles.

The growing number of rallies being organised led to an editorial article in *Buses* magazine as early as October 1971 discussing such matters as sponsorship, clashes of dates, and age limits on entrants.

An interesting 'one-off' event was an indoor 'Vintage Commercial Motor Show' at Harrogate organised by the HCVC (Yorkshire Section) and Harrogate Corporation in April 1971. This featured thirty vehicles on display including seven buses, plus enthusiast club stands, photo displays etc. Over 9,000 visitors attended the week-long event.

Events like the HCVC Runs were of course for all commercial vehicles, not just buses. Similarly, there were general vehicle rallies and road runs which featured some buses alongside cars, motorbikes, fire engines etc. Buses and other vehicles might also be displayed at the growing number of traction engine rallies. The Bluebell Railway also started a vintage transport weekend in 1966.

Most of the early rallies were static affairs on site, although there would often also be a road run preceding this. The entrants would be grouped into classes and after arrival there would be judging and prize-giving following the pattern of the HCVC London-Brighton Run. There would not normally be any opportunity for the public to ride on the vehicles unless there was a free bus link provided to the site as was the case with Showbus from Uxbridge station (modern vehicles) or Cobham Bus Museum from Weybridge station and the Lincoln Museum from the city centre (preserved vehicles from their collections).

Bus preservation can be an expensive hobby, and the initial purchase price is just the beginning! Unfortunately, many vehicles that have been saved have subsequently been scrapped or cut up for spares as their restoration proved too costly. These days there are professional companies that will undertake restoration work but in the early days it was individuals and groups learning by trial and error, often in primitive conditions. Their completed efforts would then be proudly exhibited and compared at rallies. The HCVC recognised that not every preservationist had equal resources and amongst the awards at Brighton was the Charles W. Banfield Challenge Cup for 'the best restoration during the past year by a Society member of limited means'.

Some of the top restorations have been to an extremely high standard and this is reflected in their value if the vehicles come up for resale. In 2014, two buses from the late Michael Banfield collection were auctioned at Bonham's and raised world auction price records for double-deck buses. A former 1922 London General S-type sold for £281,500 while a 1922 Tilling-Stevens TS3A sold for £216,540. Both buses were subsequently placed on loan to the London Bus Museum at Brooklands by their new owner.

I started taking photographs in 1969, attended my first HCVC Brighton run in 1971 (and have visited every year it has been held since) and visited other rallies from the early 1970s onwards. Some of these would go on to become the established rallies of today such as Showbus while others have faded into history. There were a few 'one-off' Open Days and rallies to mark notable anniversaries – something that has become more prevalent since. But there were not yet the Running Days carrying passengers over old routes that are part of today's scene – that would be a development for the future. This was largely due to the legislation of the day which prevented the taking of fares or donations for rides unless the vehicle was fully licensed and insured and the driver held a full PSV licence. While some rallies charged an admission fee, part of which might go to vehicle owners to help cover their costs, others like Southsea were free.

In this selection I have endeavoured to include many of the vehicles that were being rallied in the 1970s but have been lost to rallying or indeed to preservation since then. The pictures are taken by me except where credited.

This book is dedicated to those individuals, named and un-named whose passion and dedication have given us the wealth of vehicles and facilities we enjoy today.

While many preserved buses and coaches were bought out of service with their original or subsequent owners, some of the older vehicles have been discovered after years lying derelict or being used as the basis of a home, chicken shed etc. These may be incomplete and will take years of restoration to bring them back to their former glory. This former Aldershot & District 1930 Tilling-Stevens B10A2, seen at the Amberley Museum in 1984 shows the mammoth task that faces the restorer.

TIMELINE OF KEY EVENTS

1925	London General Omnibus Company retains examples of vehicles including horse buses and a B type motor bus.
1929	100 years of buses in London celebrated. Replica Shillibeer horse bus constructed
1933	London Transport formed and continues LGOC retention policy
1948	Southampton tram 45 is first tram to be privately preserved when bought by the Light Railway Transport League (later Light Rail Transport Association)
1955	Tramway Museum Society formed
1956	London Transport T31 becomes the first bus to be privately preserved when bought by Prince Marshall et al.
1956	1938 Exeter Leyland TS8 becomes the first bus bought by Colin Shears, founder of the West of England Collection at Winkleigh, Devon
Apr 1956	First British Coach Rally at Brighton – four preserved vehicles attended
1958	Historic Commercial Vehicle Club formed
May 1958	First HCVC event at Leyland – three buses attended
Sep 1958	HCVC event at AEC Ltd., Southall – sixteen buses attended
1959	HCVC event at the works of Harold Wood & Sons Ltd., Basildon
c.1959	Vintage Passenger Vehicle Society formed
Apr 1959	Lincolnshire Vintage Vehicle Society formed
Sep 1960	Vintage Passenger Vehicle Society rally at Hatfield, Herts.
1960	First Lincolnshire Vintage Vehicle Society display at Skellingthorpe Airfield
Jun 1961	HCVC event at the Montagu Motor Museum, Beaulieu
29.3.1961	First part of the Museum of British Transport opened
1.4.1961	Reading Transport Society formed
Sep 1961	Reading No. 113 is the first trolleybus to be privately preserved when bought by the Reading Transport Society.
May 1962	First HCVC London-Brighton Run
1962	A total of 61 privately preserved buses recorded – all built pre-war
1962	*Vintage Commercial* monthly magazine launched.
1962	Vintage Passenger Vehicle Society subsumed into the HCVC
1962	Land Transport Gallery opened at the Science Museum, London
29.5.1963	The Main Hall of the Museum of British Transport opened
Nov 1963	National Trolleybus Association formed
1965	East Anglia Transport Museum, Carlton Colville started
1966	London Bus Preservation Group founded
15.8.1968	Halifax Passenger Transport 70 years rally and gala day procession – some 30 vehicles attended
1968	Sandtoft Transport Centre Association formed
1968	First Crich Grand Transport Extravaganza
15.6.1969	First Rochdale motorcade to mark the end of municipal operators absorbed into SELNEC
Aug 1969	First HCVC Trans-Pennine Run
31.5.1970	First Bus of Yesteryear Rally, Stratford-upon-Avon
1970	Former London General B43 transferred to the Imperial War Museum
10.1.1971	First operating trolleybus at East Anglia Transport Museum, Carlton Colville
Apr 1971	HCVC 'Vintage Commercial Motor Show', Harrogate
25.4.1971	First Godalming Gathering, organised by the Vintage Transport Association
23.5.1971	Bus of Yesteryear Rally, London

4.7.1971	First Weymouth Bus Rally
11.7.1971	First rally at Eastbourne – Vintage Transport '71, organised by ELPG Enterprises (Eastbourne Lion Preservation Group)
9.10.1971	Open Day at SELNEC Stockport garage with current and preserved vehicles
1971	First Sandtoft Open Day
1971	Eastern National Preservation Group formed
29.4.1972	First rally at Bangor, Co Down, Northern Ireland
21.5.1972	Bus of Yesteryear Rally, London
1972	Cobham museum building acquired by the London Bus Preservation Group
1972	Former LGOC ST922 hired by London Transport for sightseeing route 100
1972	Former LGOC D142 hired by the English Tourist Board for a publicity tour
1972	First HCVC Bournemouth-Bath run
Jan 1973	First public opening of LBPG Cobham museum building.
21.1.1973	'Brunelzeebub' Festival Rally at Brunel University – predecessor to Showbus
23.4.1973	Museum of British Transport closed
23.5.1973	London Transport Collection at Syon Park opened
10.6.1973	First Southsea Rally, organised by the Vintage Transport Association
9.9.1973	Bradford City Transport cavalcade and open day at Thornbury overhaul works
1973	First Southport-Blackpool run organised by the Ribble Enthusiasts' Club
1973	Wiring for trolleybuses energised at Sandtoft
31.3.1974	Southport to St. Helens Run to mark these two fleets being absorbed into Merseyside PTE
6.4.1974	First Cobham Open Day
Jun 1974	Bristol Centenary Bus Rally at the BAC car park, Filton
9.6.1974	First Rykneld Run – Burton upon Trent to Derby
22/23.6.1974	'Brunelzebus' Festival Rally replaced by Showbus at the Hillingdon Show
23.6.1974	First South Essex Vintage Bus Rally at Southchurch Park, Southend
28.7.1974	Leicester City Transport Open Day to mark fifty years of motorbus operation
1974	Birmingham Museum of Transport Society formed
1976	First edition of *Preserved Buses* book by Keith A. Jenkinson
May 1978	HCVC London-Brighton Run sponsored by Foden (until 1981)
17.9.78	London Transport Collection at Syon Park closed
1978	Birmingham & Midland Motor Omnibus Trust (BaMMOT) formed and acquires site for a museum building at Wythall. Birmingham Museum of Transport Society and Birmingham Omnibus Preservation Society replaced by this.
1978	Second edition of *Preserved Buses* book by Keith A. Jenkinson – over 1,500 vehicles listed
24.6.1979	Last time that Showbus held at Uxbridge
1979	150 years of London Buses events
1980	London Transport Museum at Covent Garden opened

MUSEUM OF BRITISH TRANSPORT: 1961–1973

In 1948, Britain's railways and part of the bus industry were nationalised. An overall body, the British Transport Commission was set up to oversee transport matters. As well as looking at current and future problems, the Commission also set up a committee to consider what to do with the relics and records acquired from the old companies. This committee reported in 1951 – 'The Preservation of Relics and Records: Report to the British Transport Commission' – and its chief recommendations were accepted. A Curator of Historic Relics was appointed with an advisory committee. The report recommended that it was not just sufficient to preserve what had happened to survive from the past. The operation was an on-going one, involving 'the gradual bringing up to date of the collection from internal sources … The Commission's museum policy should therefore provide for the retention of appropriate items for the collection while they are still readily available'. A list was drawn up of machines and equipment still in service of sufficient merit to be earmarked for preservation when withdrawn.

The 1951 report recommended that the existing railway museum at York should be retained, and two others created, one in London and one in Edinburgh, with a third to be opened in Cardiff at a later date. These would not just be railway museums, but also cover a wider spectrum of road public transport and canal transport i.e. the full remit of the British Transport Commission. It would be necessary to find suitable sites for these museums. For London, the old station at Nine Elms was proposed, but this proved impractical. Then, in May-June 1958 a seven-week strike by London busmen over pay led to a decision by London Transport to make widespread service cuts to save on costs. A number of bus routes were withdrawn, or reduced in frequency, and some garages closed. Amongst the garages closed was that at Clapham in November 1958. This garage, sited in Clapham High Street, had started out as a horse tram depot in 1885, being converted to house electric trams from 1903. With the post-war tram conversion programme, the depot received its first buses in October 1950, and was fully converted to buses in January 1951. Now with closure coming a mere seven years later, Clapham was chosen as the site for a London transport museum.

John Scholes was Curator of Historical Relics and had an Advisory Panel to advise on the selection of suitable material and artefacts. The policy of the museum was to restore preserved items, as far as possible to original condition.

The museum opened in two stages, and the first, the small exhibits section, opened in the two-storey administration block on 29 March 1961. It was divided into six galleries, featuring models, paintings, maps, tickets, uniforms and other miscellanea. One gallery was entitled 'London on wheels'. In the rear yard, some of the pre-war buses saved by London Transport, of K, S and NS types were displayed at the time.

The main hall was not then open to the public but was used to store a number of vehicles including Ipswich trolleybus No. 44, Brighton, Hove & District trolleybus 6340 and London Trolleybus 260 which had been chosen by LT to be preserved as a representative London trolleybus. Ken Blacker as advisor from the HCVC considered that trolleybus 260 was not the most suitable as it had been fitted with a post-war staircase. K2 class No. 1253 was chosen instead along with Q1 class No. 1768 to represent the final class of trolleybuses. No. 260 was then destined for scrapping by George Cohen's 600 Group, but two members of the Reading Transport Society, Tony Belton and Fred Ivey, heard about this and intervened to purchase the trolleybus for £125.

The main hall opened on 29 May 1963 with 35,000sq ft available for large exhibits. Outside the main entrance, a full-size replica of Stephenson's *Rocket* greeted visitors, whilst inside there was a range of rail and road exhibits. There were fifteen railway locomotives including, as pride of place as the world speed record holder, the Gresley A4 Pacific *Mallard*, displayed with the LNER dynamometer car that recorded the record run. Other railway locos included an 1846 Furness Railway 0-4-0 *Coppernob* which had previously been on display at Barrow-in-Furness station, and still had shrapnel holes in its firebox casing, sustained in a wartime bomb attack on the station. More familiar to Londoners of an earlier generation, there was the last E4 class 2-4-0 from the former Great Eastern Railway and a 'Terrier' 0-6-0T *Boxhill* from the London, Brighton & South Coast Railway. London Transport provided the 1866 Beyer Peacock 4-4-0T No. 23 now restored to original condition with open cab, and an 1872 Aveling & Porter chain drive geared 0-4-0 originally from the Wotton Tramway. Other railway exhibits included thirteen passenger coaches, assorted wagons, signalling equipment, cast signs, nameplates and headboards.

As well as the railway exhibits, the new hall also housed the collection of buses, trolleybuses and trams that London Transport had by now amassed. There were the horse buses. Motor buses included the B type B 340 of 1911, 1920 K type K 424, 1923 S type S 742, 1931 AEC Regent ST 821, and 1930 AEC Regal T 219 in Green Line livery. There was the first production trolleybus for London, the 'Diddler' No. 1. Built in 1931 for London United, which was absorbed into London Transport in 1933, this had been retained in working order and was run in service on the last day of London trolleybuses, 8 May 1962.

London's trams had ended ten years earlier in 1952. An example of the London County Council E1 type, 1908 built No.1025 was saved and restored to 1948 condition. Trams such as this would have operated out of Clapham during its days as a tram depot. There was also a former County Borough of West Ham tram and a former London 'Feltham' tram in the colours of its subsequent owner Leeds Corporation.

LCC restrictions on museum gangway width reduced the expected space available for road vehicles. Consequently, there were no non-London buses on display inside, although there was the chassis of a 1923 Tilling-Stevens petrol-electric vehicle. There was an Ipswich trolleybus, horse trams from Chesterfield and Douglas, and electric trams from Glasgow, Douglas Southern Electric Tramways, and Llandudno & Colwyn Bay (originally Bournemouth).

The Museum of British Transport was something of a misnomer in that it only covered road and rail public transport – the intended coverage of canals never happened, and other forms of transport such as aviation and shipping were outside its remit. Notwithstanding, Clapham was a fine collection and a popular day out for families and school parties. Admission in 1963 cost 2/6d for adults and 1/6d for children.

The Transport Act 1968 created the National Bus Company and the Passenger Transport Executives. Amongst its other provisions was an allowance for the British Railways Board to transfer responsibility for its relics and records to the Department of Education & Science, which in this context meant the Science Museum. Furthermore, the BRB would find and provide, in consultation with the Science Museum, a site for a new National Railway Museum. Eventually, the

Museum of British Transport Poster.

former York North motive power depot was selected and rebuilt for its new role. One advantage claimed for York was that, with its two turntables and being rail connected, stock could be readily interchanged with a reserve collection, as it was not possible to display the whole collection at any one time. Lack of expansion space and inflexibility had been a problem at Clapham. Some of the items earmarked for preservation had still been in service at the time the museum opened and being unable to be exhibited, had had to be placed in store at various locations.

The Museum of British Transport was closed on 23 April 1973, in preparation for the removal of stock to York. The new National Railway Museum was opened by HRH The Duke of Edinburgh on 27 September 1975, 150 years after the opening of the Stockton & Darlington Railway.

But York was specifically a railway museum, and that left the road exhibits to find new homes. The provincial road exhibits from Clapham were mostly passed to the National Tramway Museum at Crich, with the Ipswich trolleybus passing to the East Anglia Transport Museum at Carlton Colville. The bulk, however, emanated from London and London Transport was determined that these, along with their former railway equipment, should stay in London. But where?

As for Clapham, the site reverted to London Transport. It was used for a while to store new and withdrawn buses. However, when Norwood bus garage was due for a total rebuild, Clapham was renovated to become an operating garage again, taking Norwood's allocation from 25 April 1981. Norwood reopened in 1984, but Streatham garage then closed for rebuilding and Clapham once again acted as host for the displaced fleet. Streatham reopened in 1987, and Clapham was finally closed. The building survived a few years as an indoor karting venue, before being demolished in 1996.

Most of the buses on display were from the London General/London Transport collection. B340 was a 1911 AEC B type with LGOC O18/16RO body, representing the first really successful mass-produced London buses. First introduced in 1910, 2,678 were built in the next three years, including single-deck versions. Over 1,000 were pressed into military service during the First World War. *Photo by Reg Batten*

MUSEUM OF BRITISH TRANSPORT: 1961–1973 • 15

Some of the other London buses on display in the main hall. On the left is S742 a 1923 AEC S type with LGOC O28/26RO body, while on the right is ST821 of 1931 an AEC Regent. The scale of progress made during the 1920s is evident with the ST now sporting a roof, enclosed staircase, a windscreen and pneumatic tyres. *Photo by Reg Batten*

The predecessors to the motor bus were not ignored with this LGOC horse bus. *Photo by Reg Batten*

As well as those saved by London Transport, some provincial trams were included. This was from The Douglas Southern Electric Tramways on the Isle of Man. After the closure of Clapham this passed to the National Tramway Museum at Crich. *Photo by Reg Batten*

The trolleybus was represented by Ipswich No. 44, a 1930 Ransomes D with Ransomes 31 seat dual-entrance body, built in Ipswich. When withdrawn in the 1950s these had been the oldest working trolleybuses in the country. No. 44 (DX 8871) was then acquired by the British Transport Commission and was displayed at Clapham. It now forms part of the Science Museum reserve collection at Wroughton following a period on loan to the East Anglia Transport Museum at Carlton Colville. *Photo by Reg Batten*

STILL IN SERVICE: 1971–2

There were still many vehicles from the 1940s or even earlier still in service at the beginning of the 1970s, including hundreds of the London Transport RT types, and several of the ubiquitous Bedford OB coaches. Some of these would last long enough to become targets for the emerging preservationists, as would many of the half-cab buses from the 1950s being replaced by one-person operated vehicles under the government bus grant scheme.

Still in use as a driver training vehicle was this 1939 built AEC Regent with Park Royal bodywork from the Salford City Transport fleet, photographed in Salford bus station on 4 September 1969. Salford would become part of SELNEC PTE (South East Lancashire & North East Cheshire) from 1 November 1969 along with most of the other municipal fleets in the Greater Manchester area. The bus survived into preservation with the Museum of Transport at Manchester. Note the message on the blind display – Dual Control Vehicle.

Perhaps the most iconic and certainly the most numerous coach was the Duple OB. First introduced in 1939, the war halted its production, but from 1945 until replaced by the SB in 1950 a total of 12,693 were built, with some 7,200 for the home market. Most had Duple bodywork. Another vehicle now in the Museum of Transport, Greater Manchester collection is HTF 586, a 1947 Bedford OB with SMT (rather than the more usual Duple) built 29 seat body new to Warburton, Bury. In March 1971 I photographed this still in service at Stratford-upon-Avon with Rouse, Oxhill, Warwickshire – his only vehicle.

18 • BUS PRESERVATION AND RALLIES: THE EARLY YEARS TO 1980

East Kent Guy Arab III FFN378 was one of five of these 1951 Park Royal bodied open-top buses hired by London Transport in 1972 to 'test the waters' for open-top vehicles on the Round London Sightseeing Tour. It is seen laying over in Piccadilly on 28 August. They were crewed by East Kent drivers and LT conductors. In 1975 London Transport would hire seven former Midland Red D9s from Obsolete Fleet, also converted to open-top and painted in LT red livery. Two of the East Kent Guys were preserved after withdrawal, as is one of the D9 open-toppers. FFN 378 was bought for preservation in 1975 but later sold and is no longer listed as preserved.

Many other vehicles were in non-PSV use with subsequent owners. One such was former Thames Valley 616, a 1952 Bristol LWL6B with ECW bodywork which when seen here at Southampton in October 1972 was being used by the Coalporters Amateur Rowing Club and had been fitted with roof racks to carry the boats. After this was replaced by the club it passed into preservation and was restored to Thames Valley livery (see p. 48)

HCVC LONDON TO BRIGHTON RUN: 2 MAY 1971

The London-Brighton Run had its beginnings when the Historic Commercial Vehicle Club (now Society) was formed in 1958 to cater for the emerging interest in preserving commercial vehicles. A first rally was organised at Leyland in May of that year, which was attended by twenty-two historic vehicles, three of which were buses. A further event was held at the premises of AEC Ltd. at Southall in September. Over forty vehicles attended this, including sixteen buses or coaches. Four of these were from London Transport's own preserved collection. Those vehicles present there were K424, NS 1995, STL 469 and Q55, all of which remain as part of their collection today, with some displayed at the museum at Covent Garden. Others were privately owned, reflecting this as yet new but growing interest. Amongst these were Gilford AS6 DX 9547, then owned by Jack Mulley and now preserved at the Bressingham Steam Museum and ex-Leicester AEC Renown CBC 921 then entered by the Vintage Passenger Vehicle Society and now with Leicestershire Museums.

A few other rallies were held over the next three or four years, such as at Beaulieu in 1961. The Montagu Motor Museum (now the National Motor Museum) had been founded at Beaulieu in 1952 by Lord Montagu as an attraction to bring in visitor income to help pay for the upkeep of the estate. It was primarily a collection of cars, but Lord Montagu was supportive of the HCVC from the outset and later became its President.

As we entered the 1960s, private preservation was growing in both momentum and credibility. Two other societies, the Vintage Passenger Vehicle Society and the London Vintage Taxi Club merged with the HCVC in 1962 to bring it to the forefront as the main voice of the movement. Some preservationists were banding together to form local societies and arrange collective covered accommodation for their vehicles. From such groupings major collections such as the Lincolnshire Vintage Vehicle Society were formed.

The first Brighton run took place in May of 1962, starting from the Museum of British Transport at Clapham and attracting over fifty vehicles. Brighton was already established as a venue for such events. There was the Veteran Car Club's run in November to commemorate the repeal of the Red Flag Act in 1896 (which still takes place). There was also the British Coach Rally, which had been held there most years since its inauguration in 1956. The run was judged to be a success, such that it was back the next year and every year since then until the Covid pandemic prevented the 2020 and 2021 events.

The Brighton run grew to feature around 200 vehicles each year. These were divided into classes. Vans and lorries were split according to load capacity and age. Then there were classes for fire engines with open and enclosed cabs, passenger vehicles with under twenty seats, single and double deck vehicles with over twenty seats, military vehicles, specialised vehicles, purpose-built taxis, and steam vehicles. On arrival at Brighton, a panel of judges inspected the entrants and there was a wide range of trophies to be awarded. This pattern has continued ever since, although the classes have been amended over the years. With high standards of restoration on display, the judge's task must at times be quite a difficult one! There is a rolling minimum age requirement for vehicles entering the run of 21 years.

The support of the city council has been an important consideration, with the mayor of Brighton on hand to present the trophies. Brighton rightly sees the HCVS run as a significant event in the town's annual calendar.

For many years, the start point for the run was Battersea Park, with entrants departing at intervals from around 6.30am. The route was mainly down the A23 with a stopover at Crawley.

The original 1962 Run was sponsored by National Benzole, who then sponsored each year until 1973. The Runs were then funded by the HCVC. Sponsorship returned in 1978 in the shape of Foden Ltd., the truck builders, whose own history dates back to 1856. The company had preserved a number of their own vehicles, both steam and diesel including their first diesel lorry of 1931, and some of these took part in the run. Foden had built passenger vehicles from time to time but had never been major players in the market. However, a few Foden buses and coaches have made it into preservation and one of these appeared at Brighton on at least two occasions. This was MTU 296, a 1948 PVFE6 with two-stroke engine and Metalcraft C37F body, new to local operator Coppenhall of Sandbach. Foden's sponsorship ended in 1981.

Former Ribble 2057 (RN 8622) a 1939 Leyland TD5 with an Alexander L27/26R body which had been fitted in 1949. This was sold in 1960 and then used as staff transport until bought for preservation in 1968.

Carrying a modern registration number and fictitious Halifax Corporation livery at the time, MJX 222J was a 1931 Leyland bodied Leyland TD1 which was formerly Jersey Motor Traction No. 24 (J 1199). This has since been given a more sympathetic 'period' UK registration as SV 6107 and has regained Jersey livery.

A more modern Leyland was former Southdown 1179 (DUF 179), a 1937 Tiger TS7 with Harrington C32R bodywork. This was one of the first vehicles to be bought for preservation in 1957 and had been entered at the HCVC event held at Basildon in 1959. The owner in 1971 hailed from Blackpool hence the 'Blackpool to Brighton' board on the radiator. DUF 179 now forms part of the large heritage fleet of Ensignbus, Purfleet.

Not so pristine at the time was GAM 215. This is former Wilts & Dorset 296, a 1950 Bristol L6B with bodywork by Portsmouth Aviation from the collection of Mr Hoare at Chepstow. Similar GAM 216 also survives in preservation.

Also not yet restored to original livery was Bedford OB LTA 750 formerly Southern National [Royal Blue] 1411. In the 2021 PSV Circle Preserved Buses list this is listed as now being with Blue Motors, Blackpool as an active heritage vehicle within their fleet. Indeed, many of the surviving Bedford OBs are with commercial operators, being ideal for wedding hires, film and promotional work etc.

Making a contrast with the British buses was this 1933 Renault TN6A series, one of the typical Paris open-back buses with STCRP bodywork and thirty-three seats. This was formerly RATP No. 2481, one of a small number of these Paris buses that were brought over to Britain for preservation.

HCVC LONDON TO BRIGHTON RUN: 7 MAY 1972

DR 4902, a 1929 Leyland Titan TD1, new to the National Omnibus & Transport Co (later Southern National). This was sold to Chivers (makers of jam) for staff transport in 1937. After withdrawal in 1955 it was painted in Eastern Counties livery and was an exhibit at the erstwhile Museum of British Transport at Clapham. In 1966, the HCVC took charge of the bus as a tender and this is now part of the Science Museum reserve collection kept at Wroughton.

Southdown 813 (UF 4813) a 1929 Leyland TDI with Brush open-top bodywork was one of the vehicles that participated in the inaugural 1962 London to Brighton run. This was retained by Southdown and passed with the company to the Stagecoach Group with whom it has been retained as part of their heritage collection.

Imported from the Isle of Man was former Douglas Corporation 50, a 1939 AEC Regent with Northern Counties H27/25R body. This had been given a UK registration SWU 222F. The bus has since returned to preservation on the Isle of Man and regained its original registration DMN 650.

Former London Transport Green Line T448, a 1936 AEC Regal with Weymann bodywork, was entered by the London Bus Preservation Trust and is the only survivor of the '9T9' class. This was rescued, engine-less, from a scrapyard in 1968. The Trust have been regular supporters of the run, entering one or more vehicles each year. In 1972 they also entered G351 (HGC 130), their wartime Guy Arab II, which had also been entered in 1968.

Ex-Burton-upon-Trent FA 9750, a 1950 Guy Arab III with Davies H30/26R bodywork at Brighton in 1972 participating in the HCVC London-Brighton Run. Bought in 1971, unfortunately this bus is no longer in preservation having been scrapped by a subsequent owner. Former London Transport T792 being admired alongside is still very much with us though and regularly rallied.

Nicely presented complete with a period advertising board is former Provincial, Leicester JF 2378, a 1931 AEC Regal with Burlingham C32R bodywork. Note the London Transport roundel on the radiator, suggesting that this may have spent a period on loan to LT during post-war shortages.

Seen parked up near the marina end of Madeira Drive was KYD 151. This is a 1949 AEC Regal III with Harrington C33F bodywork, new to Scarlet & Blue, Minehead and later owned by Prince Coach Tours, Cardiff. Purchased for preservation by D. Hoare and entered as acquired, it would be back in later years fully repainted (see p. 81).

PRESERVED LONDON BUSES BACK IN USE: 1972

From 8 April to 27 October 1972, for the first time London Transport hired a preserved bus to work a scheduled route. Former Tilling and later General 1930 AEC Regent ST922 was hired from Obsolete Fleet. It ran daily on a circular route 100 from Horse Guards Avenue and was sponsored by Johnnie Walker whisky, whose adverts it carried. The bus had been bought for preservation by Prince Marshall in 1966 and stored until 1971 when it was renovated by LPC Coachworks Ltd. ST922 was hired again in 1973 although the routing was altered. It also ran each summer until at least 1977, in which year the route 100 ran between Trafalgar Square and the Tower of London. Each year it ran it was sponsored by different companies whose products it advertised.

An even older London General bus also took to the road in 1972. D142, a 1925 Dennis 3-ton chassis with Dodson open-top body was acquired by the LGOC from the London Public Omnibus Company in 1929. Later converted to pneumatic tyres it was withdrawn in 1932. The body was found in the garden of a smallholding in 1970 where it had languished for some thirty-five years. Restoration by LPC Coachworks Ltd. for Prince Marshall, Chairman of the London Bus Preservation Group, was completed by February 1972. The bus was then sent on a five-week tour of England sponsored by the English Tourist Board distributing tourism brochures. (for photo see p. 116)

A third ex-London vehicle on the roads in 1972 was Inter-Station Leyland Cub CLX 548 which toured London railway termini in connection with the launch of *History of Railways* by the New English Library. (for photo see p. 117)

ST922 is seen in Horse Guards Avenue on 15 April 1972 while working on route 100.

HCVC LONDON TO BRIGHTON RUN: 1973

One of the strangest vehicles to have been entered at Brighton! Thames Ironworks were shipbuilders, best known for the preserved HMS *Warrior*, but from 1911 to 1913 they began producing a passenger vehicle. Resembling a horseless carriage this had solid front wheels of 3ft diameter and rear wheels of 4ft 4in diameter. Power was provided by a 40hp six-cylinder petrol engine. XM 215 was new to Universal, London and has bodywork built by Thrupp & Maberley. Eight passengers were carried inside and another sixteen precariously seated on top. At the time, this unique machine was at the National Motor Museum, Beaulieu, but is now preserved at a museum in Holland. It was also exhibited at the First Brighton Coach Rally in 1956.

Also at Brighton in 1973 was JA 7591 a 1936 Leyland Tiger TS7 with English Electric B35C bodywork ex-Stockport 191. This was from the growing collection of Mr Hoare, Chepstow. It was lettered for its last working use with Stockport's Welfare Department.

LONDON TRANSPORT COLLECTION, SYON PARK: 1973

With the announcement that the Museum of British Transport would be closing as a result of the rail exhibits moving to the new National Railway Museum at York, there was a determination to retain the London Transport exhibits at a location in London. During 1971, one location promoted by the Transport Trust to the government was for a museum to be constructed above the Southern Region station at Crystal Palace (low level). This would provide a floor space of 4,000sq ft and be rail connected to central London.

This did not materialise and following the closure of the Museum of British Transport on 23 April 1973, a new site was instead quickly found at Syon Park, near Brentford in west London. This became known as the new London Transport Collection and opened on 23 May 1973, being formally declared open by the Duke of Northumberland, owner of Syon Park. The site was managed by the Syon Park authorities on behalf of London Transport. The single storey hall housed all the London exhibits from Clapham, and seven other vehicles for which space had been previously unavailable. The full list of vehicles displayed at Syon Park was as follows: double deck buses B340, K424, LT165, NS1995, ST821, STL469; single deck buses Q 55, T219, TF 77, plus the Tilling-Stevens petrol electric chassis. Also on display were trolleybuses 'Diddler' No.1, K1 class 1253, Q1 class 1768. There were three trams: ex-West Ham No. 290; LCC E1 type No. 1025 and Metropolitan Electric Tramways 'Feltham' car No. 355. There was also the truck of an LCC HR2 type tram. There was the replica Shillibeer horse bus, Tilling knifeboard horse bus, and LGOC garden-seat horse bus. Railway exhibits comprised the Metropolitan 4-4-0T No. 23, the Aveling & Porter geared loco, Metropolitan electric loco No. 5 *John Hampden* and a Q23 type motor car from the District line. Showcases and poster displays lined the side walls. Unlike Clapham, with its wide aisles, space at Syon Park was at a premium, making photography of many of the exhibits a difficult feat. By the end of the year there had been some 75,000 visitors.

Although successful, the Syon Park site lacked further expansion space. More crucially, it was considered too remote from the passing tourist trade. Therefore, London Transport remained on the lookout for other alternative premises in a more central location.

London Transport Collection, Syon Park poster

LONDON TRANSPORT COLLECTION, SYON PARK: 1973 • 31

Space was rather restricted within Syon Park making photography somewhat difficult. Here we have T219 the 1931 AEC Regal with Duple body in Green Line livery. This had previously been at Clapham and before that had been entered in the inaugural 1962 HCVC London – Brighton Run. Behind it is TF77 (FJJ 774) which had not been previously exhibited at Clapham. Photographed in 1977

Amongst the double-deckers was ST821 (GK 3192) which was depicted earlier at Clapham.

SOUTHSEA RALLY: 10 JUNE 1973

The first Southsea Rally took place at the Southsea Castle car park on 10 June 1973. This was organised by the Vintage Transport Association and was the successor to two earlier Godalming Gathering events held in 1971-2. It was arranged in conjunction with the City Museums Department of Portsmouth Corporation and entitled Southsea Spectacular. There were some fifty or so entrants in classes of pre-1950, post-1950 and modern vehicles.

Former Southdown 547 (PUF 647) a 1956 Guy Arab IV with Park Royal bodywork was in attendance having been purchased for preservation after further service with Confidence of Oadby, Leicestershire.

ENT 778, a 1948 Leyland Tiger PS1 with Burlingham C33F bodywork, was new to Gittins, Crickheath, but was presented in the colours of later operator Premier-Albanian, Watford who had retained the vehicle and restored it to mark their 50th Anniversary.

A rare vehicle which attended at Southsea was this Sentinel SLC4 with Beadle DP41F bodywork ex-Brown, Donnington Wood. In the 1930s, Sentinel had been a major maker of 'undertype' steam lorries featuring an underfloor engine and they kept this arrangement when they went over to building diesel lorries and coaches. Production only lasted from 1950 to 1954. This is a vehicle which I have not seen since this occasion.

WEYMOUTH RALLY: 1 JULY 1973

The first Weymouth Bus Rally was held on 4 July 1971 at the Seafront Coach Park, Lodmoor, Weymouth. This was organised by the Dorset Transport Circle and Weymouth Model Engineers. A feature was a 20-mile round trip road run for the vehicles to the Isle of Portland. The format was repeated in 1972. I first visited the Weymouth Rally on 1 July 1973. More than seventy vehicles were entered and most of these were able to attend.

Right: Weymouth Rally 1971 advert

Below: Entered by the Bristol Tramways Vintage Bus Group, GHT 154 is a 1940 Bristol K5G with Bristol (BBW) bodywork. This had been cut down to open top during subsequent use by a showman, but the preservation group have since rebuilt the upper deck.

Being in Southern National territory, not surprisingly there were a number of former vehicles from the company entered including these two Royal Blue coaches. 1291 (MOD 978) is a 1952 Bristol LS6G while 2200 (OTT 43) dates from 1953, both with ECW bodywork.

An earlier generation of Royal Blue coaches is represented by 1250 (LTA 729), a 1951 LL6B with Duple C37F bodywork. This was bought from a scrap dealer by Colin Shears in 1968 and sold on to Colin Billington in 1972. Note that both this and 1291 have additional provision for carrying luggage on the roof.

BUS OF YESTERYEAR RALLY, CLAPHAM COMMON: 15–16 SEPTEMBER 1973

The Bus of Yesteryear Rally organised by the London Bus Preservation Group first took place at Stratford-upon-Avon in May 1970. The rallies of May 1971 and 1972 were held in London on the South Bank and Somers Town goods yard respectively. In 1973 it moved to a weekend in September on Clapham Common. This was to form part of the London Autumn Trades Fair sponsored by the South London Press. As well as buses, the event featured preserved cars, commercials, motorcycles and traction engines.

Advert in *Buses* magazine for The Bus of Yesteryear Rally 1971

Advert in *Buses* magazine for the The Bus of Yesteryear Rally 1970

Advert in *Buses* magazine for the Bus of Yesteryear Rally 1973

Amongst the PSVs at Clapham was NXL 847 the 1953 AEC Regal III with Duple C39F body from Eastern Belle of Bow – one of the last half-cab coaches to work for a London operator. Preserved initially by John Brenson in Essex, this is now part of the extensive collection of Roger Burdett and resides in the West Midlands area.

Former London Transport 738J, an STL class 1933 AEC Regent which was one of a number rebodied by Chalmers in 1950 to become breakdown tenders. Alongside is STL2692, a 1946 AEC Regent II/Weymann H30/26R which saw subsequent service with Grimsby Cleethorpes Corporation.

HCVC LONDON TO BRIGHTON RUN: 5 MAY 1974

JUB 29 is a very early Leyland TD1 of 1928 but this was rebodied in 1951 with a 1932 Eastern Counties body. Keighley-West Yorkshire K451 was originally Glasgow 72 and first registered GE 2407. It had passed to Wallace Arnold in 1944 who had re-registered it. Owned by Keith Jenkinson from West Yorkshire, this was awarded a cup for the vehicle travelling the furthest distance to the run under its own power. 'The vehicle just visible on the left is also a Leyland'.

HWO 334 is a 1949 Guy Arab III with Duple L27/26RD bodywork. This was new to Red & White as their L1149 but was liveried here for subsequent owners Provincial (Gosport & Fareham). This was first bought for preservation by Mr D. Fereday Glenn who preserved a number of buses from Hampshire companies from 1968 onwards. The Guy is now with BaMMOT at the Transport Museum, Whythall and back in Red & White colours. Alongside is ex-Gelligaer 19 (MTG 84) a 1953 AEC Regal III with Longwell Green bodywork. This is now part of the National Museum of Wales collection.

BG 8557 is a 1944 Arab II of Birkenhead Corporation. Originally it would have carried a wartime-built utility body, but it was rebodied in 1953 by Massey Bros. This was withdrawn in 1967 and preserved in 1969. As it was parked away from the rally area it was possibly not an entrant but just visiting. A Bedford OB with Duple body can be seen behind. This is MHU 992 ex-Bristol Omnibus 220.

Also 'just visiting' were not one but two ex-London Transport TDs. TD89, a 1949 Leyland PS1 with Mann Egerton bodywork is seen, and behind it is the more familiar TD95 (JXC 288) from the London Bus Preservation Trust at Cobham. This was probably attending as a tender vehicle for Dennis D142 (XX 9591) which was a Run entrant.

A feature of the Brighton Runs in the mid-1970s was the number of visiting preserved vehicles that were not official entrants. These tended to park up in back streets, particularly around by the Southdown (ex-Brighton, Hove & District) Whitehawk garage. Seen in 1974 was former Barton 467 (JNN 384), a 1947 Leyland PD1 with Duple lowbridge front-entrance body to Barton specification.

LEICESTER OPEN DAY: 28 JULY 1974

On 28 July 1974, Leicester City Transport held an Open Day at their Abbey Park Road depot to mark fifty years of motor bus operation. Many visiting preserved vehicles were on display as well as examples from their own fleet, past and present.

Right: Leicester open day 1974 advert

Below: Amongst former Leicester vehicles was 246, an all-Leyland PD1 of 1946, latterly Barton No. 847. This does not appear to have survived to the present day, but similar 248 (DJF 349) is now with the GC Heritage Trust at Ruddington.

LEICESTER CITY TRANSPORT
celebrate their
50th ANNIVERSARY OF MOTORBUS OPERATION
on 24th July, 1974.
Special events include
- Fully illustrated brochure on sale.
- Sunday July 21 to Sunday July 28, special bus service along the first bus route operated by a bus repainted in 1924 livery—souvenir tickets issued.
- Wednesday July 24, first day postal cover on sale at Rutland Street operating centre; postal facilities provided.
- Sunday July 28, open day at Abbey Park Road depot:-
    photographic and film display
    preserved vehicles on display
    depot and workshops open
    commemorative service extended to Abbey Park Road.

For full details send SAE to:-
    The General Manager,
    50 Year Celebrations,
    Leicester City Transport,
    Abbey Park Road,
    Leicester LE4 5AH

LEICESTER OPEN DAY: 28 JULY 1974 • 41

Also from Barton was No. 49. NNN 968 is a Barton BTS1, one of a number of vehicles they rebuilt themselves in the late 1940s/early 1950s from pre-war chassis. Originally numbered 668 it was later rebuilt again to become a transporter for their preserved 1923 Daimler charabanc W913 (originally NW 7341) which was fitted with a replica body in 1953 to represent the Durham Churchill with which they started business in 1908. This is seen on the back of the transporter. Both vehicles are now part of the Barton Cherished Vehicle Collection.

Blue Bus Services of Willington were the original operators of GNU 750, a 1939 Daimler COG5/40 with Willowbrook C35F body. After withdrawal in 1965 it passed through several preservationist owners. In the 1990s it was owned by coach company Jeffs of Helmdon but is no longer listed as being in preservation.

LRB 750 is a 1948 Bedford OB from the fleet of Booth & Fisher, Halfway, near Sheffield. Unusually it does not have the customary Duple bodywork but was bodied by Barnaby. A vehicle I have never seen again since this occasion.

KKH 650 is a 1949 AEC Regal III with Weymann bodywork ex-Kingston-upon-Hull. This is now owned by the Hull Museums Department and is a static exhibit at the Hull Streetlife Museum of Transport.

Leaving for home is the well-known former West Bromwich No. 32, a Dennis ES of 1929. Fitted with a Dixon B32F body this has been with the 32 Group, Birmingham since 1964.

Originating from much further away was ex-Portsmouth 5. RV 6358 is one of four from a batch of 1935 Leyland TD4s with English Electric bodies that were converted to open-top for the summer seafront service to Hayling Ferry. They were not replaced until 1971-2 and all passed into preservation. RV 6358 has since been rebuilt with a removable upper deck in preservation.

HCVC LONDON TO BRIGHTON RUN: 4 MAY 1975

KEL 133: one of the famous Bournemouth double-deckers with dual entrance/exit and two staircases – a feature that was also specified on their trolleybuses. This is a 1950 Leyland PD2/3 with Weymann bodywork. Four of this batch are preserved.

This was another year when a variety of interesting vehicles could be found parked around the back streets. Leading is KCF 711, a 1957 Guy Arab IV with Roe bodywork new to Chambers of Bures, Suffolk. This is a vehicle I have never seen since although it is still listed as preserved. Behind it is PTW 110, the 1951 Bristol L6B/ECW ex-Eastern National 4107 with the Eastern National Preservation Group.

Seen parked up in a coach park was former Southdown 764, a 1953 Leyland PD2/12 with Northern Counties H56RD bodywork. Although looking in fine condition here, this is another vehicle that later dropped out of preservation.

SOUTHSEA RALLY: 8 JUNE 1975

One entry at Southsea in 1975 was VH 6217. This is a 1934 AEC Regent, originally a Huddersfield bus, but converted to a tower wagon and acquired by Bournemouth. This was part of the Bournemouth Heritage Transport Collection but has since been sold and is reported to be with an owner in Dundee.

Also at Southsea was CDL 792, a 1939 Bedford WTB with Duple bodywork, ex-Shotter, Brighstone, Isle of Wight.

46 • BUS PRESERVATION AND RALLIES: THE EARLY YEARS TO 1980

Posed in the sun was former Aldershot & District 178 (HOU 904), a 1950 Dennis Lancet III with Strachan B38R bodywork. Aldershot & District bought mostly Dennis vehicles as they were built locally at Guildford. This remained in service until 1967 and was preserved in 1971.

Seen posing with an impressive selection of awards is the former City of Oxford 703, a 1949 AEC Regal III with Willowbrook DP32F bodywork, owned and entered by the Oxford Bus Museum Trust.

SHOWBUS RALLY – UXBRIDGE: 28–29 JUNE 1975

The most significant new rally happened almost by accident when Martin Isles, Chairman of Brunel University's Omnibus Society was asked what they would be doing for Brunelzeebub, the University's Community Festival in January 1973. He suggested asking London Transport if they would bring a (then new) DMS bus, but this was misunderstood and publicised as bringing a vintage bus, and so the idea of a bus rally was born. An approach to the London Bus Preservation Group and an advert in *Buses* magazine produced a few preserved vehicles, but others had been delicensed for winter, so to supplement the total local operators were invited and some brought their latest vehicles. A total of eleven vehicles attended (six preserved, five current) and there was a parade around the site. A second Brunelzebus Rally was planned for February 1974, but this was postponed because of national economic problems. It instead became part of the Hillingdon Borough Show at Uxbridge Showground on 22-23 June and hence was renamed Showbus. This featured a road run to Windsor and back on the Sunday. Nearly 100 vehicles were entered. From these modest beginnings would come the largest annual bus rally, which is still going strong in 2021, and still organised by Dr Martin Isles. I first went to the 1975 rally, held again at Uxbridge. This had sponsorship from National Travel South East and again featured a road run to Windsor and back.

Brunelzeebub Rally 1973 advert

Brunelzebus Rally 1974 advert

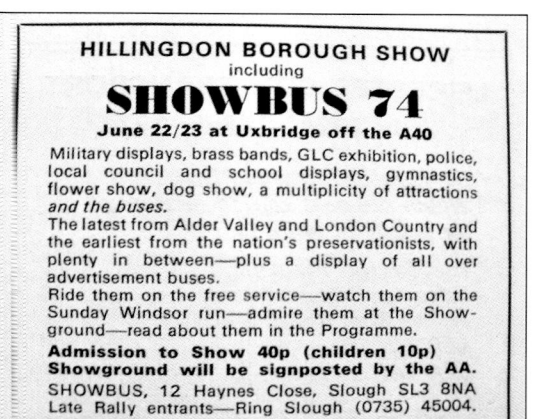

Showbus Rally 1974 advert

Showbus Rally 1975 advert

Looking resplendent was Former Thames Valley Bristol LWL6B 616 (GJB 254) now with the Egham Bus Group. Contrast this with the picture before preservation (see p. 18)

Recently acquired by the Eastern National Preservation Group was the ex-Moores, Kelvedon 1963 Guy Arab IV with Massey bodywork 373 WPU. Moores had been taken over by Eastern National in 1963 and the Guy had become No. 2017 in their fleet.

SHOWBUS RALLY – UXBRIDGE: 28–29 JUNE 1975 • **49**

London vehicles dominate this view. Pride of place is STL2692 of 1946. This batch of post-war AEC Regent II STLs for the country area had Weymann H30/26R bodies. STL2692 was sold to Grimsby Corporation in 1955 and on withdrawal by Grimsby-Cleethorpes in 1968 was bought for preservation, being entered on the 1968 London-Brighton Run.

It wasn't just preserved buses at Uxbridge. Showbus has always been about showcasing modern buses as well as preserved vehicles. London Country Leyland Atlantean AN96 in overall advertising livery was used on the shuttle service from Uxbridge station, London & Manchester Assurance being one of the sponsors. Alongside is London Transport's unique rear engine Routemaster FRM1, then in service but eventually destined for preservation by the London Transport Museum.

RUSHMOOR ARENA RALLY: 20 JULY 1975

Rushmoor Arena was an Army owned site near Aldershot. I saw this event advertised in *Buses* magazine. It was billed as 'The Yesteryear Show'. Entries were invited for preserved buses, commercials, traction engines, etc to appear at this 'new event in the largest arena in the South'. All proceeds were to go to charity. A vintage bus service connected the site with Aldershot bus station. Following the success of this the 'Rushmoor Steam and Vintage Show' started in 1978, organised by the Three Counties Steam Preservation Society. This continued each year until 1995 with some buses and other commercials attending, and then a final rally in 1998. These rallies then ceased when the Army closed the site in a round of spending cuts.

Some of the preserved buses can be seen here. GLJ 964 was a 1947 Bristol K5G which was rebodied by owners Hants & Dorset c.1957 as an open-topper. Sadly, this no longer survives, but similar GLJ 971 is still preserved.

Former East Kent FFN 378, a 1951 Guy Arab III with Park Royal body converted to open-top. In 1972 this had been one of five similar buses hired by London Transport for the Round London Sightseeing Tour (see p. 18). After withdrawal by East Kent, FFN 378 was bought by Mr Fereday Glenn for preservation but was reported as exported in 1976. Similar FFN 382 however still survives.

The massive radiator indicates that this is a Daimler CD650DD, from the fleet of Blue Bus Services, Willington. The lowbridge bodywork is by Willowbrook. Sister SRB 424 is also preserved, in the Coventry Transport Museum.

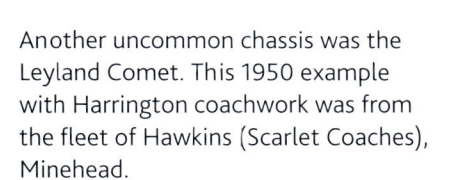

Another uncommon chassis was the Leyland Comet. This 1950 example with Harrington coachwork was from the fleet of Hawkins (Scarlet Coaches), Minehead.

PRESERVATION SITES AND VEHICLES IN THE MID 1970s

For many preservationists, a major problem was finding covered accommodation for their vehicles. Some, perhaps working for bus companies, were able to keep vehicles at bus garages. If vehicles were kept on non-secure sites, there was a danger of vandalism, and unfortunately some vehicles were lost to arson or vandalism. Collective preservation groups were set up and in some cases were able to acquire redundant bus garage sites as museum buildings, such as the Eastern National Preservation Group at Canvey Island.

EAP 4 was a 1948 Bristol K5G from Brighton, Hove & District that had been converted to a towing lorry, and later passed to Southdown. This was photographed near Hove garage in 1975 having been restored to BH&D livery. This was later at a site in Woolwich in 1978 (see p. 100) but I believe this became a victim of arson and lost to the preservation movement.

The W4 Preservation Society also owned HJG 21, a former East Kent 1954 Dennis Lancet UF with Duple C41C body. This was also seen stored in the open opposite Hove garage in 1976. This also no longer exists so probably suffered a similar fate.

PRESERVATION SITES AND VEHICLES IN THE MID 1970s • 53

Continental Pioneer were a coach company from Richmond, Surrey. They also operated a former local London Transport bus route, the 235. Their yard was home to a variety of vehicles undergoing preservation, which seemed to be different on every visit I made. On 19 January 1975 I encountered LRA 907, a 1947 AEC Regal III with Duple body ex-Silver Service, Darley Dale near Matlock. This was keeping company with a pair of London Transport RTLs which had subsequently seen service in Jersey, seen behind, and another RT family bus.

A year later, in January 1976, former Jersey 1959 Leyland PD2/31 No. 16 J 1583 with Reading bodywork was in their yard with more London RTs.

54 • BUS PRESERVATION AND RALLIES: THE EARLY YEARS TO 1980

In May 1976 a visit revealed JFJ 606, a 1949 Daimler CVD6 with Brush bodywork, formerly Exeter No. 43. Alongside is LFJ 931 a single-deck Daimler CVD6 with Duple C37F body from the fleet of Greenslades, Exeter. This latter vehicle was reported as sold to breakers in 1992.

Looking rather sorry for itself in the yard of Golden Boy Coaches at Roydon in 1976 was ex-London Transport RT1062 (JXN 90) of 1948 with Saunders bodywork. This had later worked for Ward, Epping. Although listed as preserved in 1993 it had dropped off the list by 1999, so probably got cut up for spares.

PRESERVATION SITES AND VEHICLES IN THE MID 1970s • 55

In Halifax in January 1976, a number of preserved vehicles were being housed in a former railway carriage shed. These included ex-Morecambe & Heysham Corporation 69 (LTF 254) 1950 AEC Regent III with Park Royal H30/26R bodywork.

At the premises of S&M Coaches, South Benfleet in April 1976 was the Eastern National Preservation Group's Bristol L5G ONO 49. This, like their other vehicles, is now kept at the former Canvey Island bus garage, now the Canvey Island Transport Museum

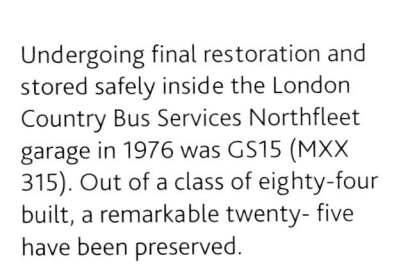

Undergoing final restoration and stored safely inside the London Country Bus Services Northfleet garage in 1976 was GS15 (MXX 315). Out of a class of eighty-four built, a remarkable twenty-five have been preserved.

HCVC LONDON TO BRIGHTON RUN: 2 MAY 1976

A classic 1930s Leyland. VD 3433 is a 1934 Lion LT5A rebodied in 1945 with an Alexander thirty-four seat body, formerly Alexander P721. This was owned and entered by Jasper Pettie from Fife in Scotland and driven all the way from there and back – over 1,000 miles. No surprise that it won the award for travelling the greatest distance. Alongside is London Transport STL2692 again.

Another Leyland, but by contrast one that had been in preservation for many years and was the veteran of many Brighton Runs. DM 6228 is a 1929 Lioness LTB1 with Burlingham body new to Brookes (White Rose), Rhyl. It later worked in Jersey until 1958 where it was registered J 2975. Then owned by Peter Stanier, this had spent some time in the 1960s in the care of Geoffrey Hilditch, general manager of Halifax Passenger Transport Department and took part in the 70 years rally held there in 1968.

In 1966, recently withdrawn Eastern National 2255 (ONO 59), a 1949 Bristol K5G, was bought for £145 by seven lads from Leigh-on-Sea, Essex and converted as a mobile home. On 27 January 1967 they set off to Europe to see how far they could go. Eventually this would lead to their becoming the first people to drive a bus right round the world, with the 'Essex Bus Boys' returning to Dover on 27 August 1969. It then became a tender vehicle for the Lincolnshire Vintage Vehicle Society, in which role it attended the 1976 Run. Later it was used by the LVVS as a static bookstore. Restoration started in 2015 and in 2018 it was finally fully restored to its Eastern National condition.

Approaching Old Steine and the seafront at the end of its journey to Brighton, LOD 495 is a 1950 Albion Victor FT39N with Duple C31F body new to Way, Crediton. This vehicle has remained in active preservation in Devon with Hazell, Northlew.

TJ 836 is a 1933 Dennis Dart with Duple twenty seat bodywork new to Entwistle, Morecambe. At this time, it was privately owned, but has since been acquired by Alexander Dennis Ltd, Guildford as part of their heritage collection. At Brighton it won the National Benzole Cup as the outright winner of the Concours D'Elegance and the British Leyland Challenge Cup for the best passenger vehicle.

LONDON TRANSPORT COLLECTION, SYON PARK: 16 MAY 1976

A Gala Day and Collectors' Sale with a small rally was held at Syon Park, home of the London Transport Collection in May 1976. Amongst the vehicles present was ex-Bristol C2736 a 1949 Bristol L5G with ECW dual-door 33 seat body. This was part of the Bristol city fleet, hence the 'C' prefix and city coat-of-arms on the side.

SOUTHEND RALLY: 6 JUNE 1976

A first South Essex Vintage Bus Rally organised by the Eastern National Preservation Group was advertised to be held in Southchurch Park, Southend on 23 June 1974. A second followed in 1975 and I first visited the 1976 rally.

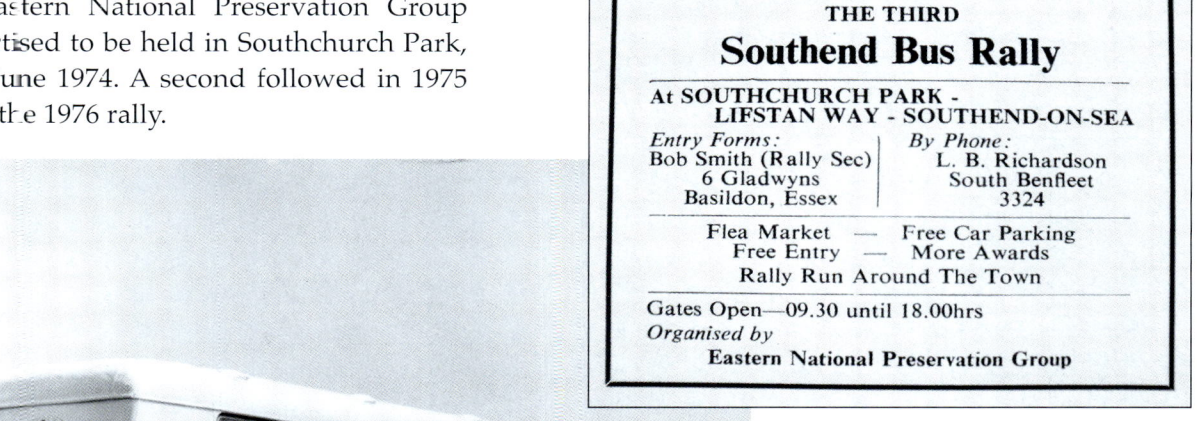

Above: Southend Rally 1976 advert

Left: GBE 846 was a 1950 Bristol K5G6, originally Lincolnshire 2136. On withdrawal it passed to Eastern National who fitted it out as a publicity vehicle and also gave it a full front and Lodekka style grille. The upper deck was fitted out as a cinema to show films of holiday tours. By 1976, when I photographed it at the Southend Bus Rally, it was owned by the East Anglian branch of the HCVC. Despite this, by 1999 it was no longer listed as being preserved.

Another entrant was BPV 9, ex-Ipswich 9, a 1953 AEC Regal IV with Park Royal dual-door bodywork. Exhibited before full repaint, this is now part of the Ipswich Transport Museum Collection.

60 • BUS PRESERVATION AND RALLIES: THE EARLY YEARS TO 1980

Two more of the entrants. CNH 862, a 1952 Bristol LWL5G ex-United Counties 862; HWW 642, a Bedford OB/Duple then owned by local company S&M, South Benfleet. This later passed to Dean, Paisley but is no longer listed in preservation.

A vehicle still very active in the Oxford Bus Museum Trust collection, AEC Regal III/Willowbrook OJO 727 made a trip to Southend to participate.

A very unusual vehicle for the area. This ex-West Riding 1963 Guy Wulfrunian WHL 970 was operated by Holman, of Crouch Hill, London N8. It retained the colours of a previous owner, McLennan, Spittalfield in Perthshire. This was probably entered by Holman as I had seen and photographed it the previous day on private hire duty at Wembley Stadium. It would later pass into the care of the West Riding Omnibus Preservation Society.

SOUTHSEA RALLY: 13 JUNE 1976

The following week it was the Southsea Rally, this time held on the Common. This vast area gave much more space allowing vehicles to be better spaced out for photography. There were approximately 130 vehicles on show and a record number of sales stands.

Pride of place has to go to Portsmouth 10 (BK 2986). This is a 1919 Thornycroft J with a c.1920 Dodson body. Portsmouth Corporation were one of the few undertakings that had put aside historic vehicles for preservation although they were not on public display. The Southsea rallies created an opportunity to put them on show. With the opening of Hampshire's Milestones Museum at Basingstoke in 2000, the Portsmouth collection including the Thornycroft and trolleybus No. 1 are now on permanent display there, posed in recreated period street settings.

Formerly in the Wilts & Dorset fleet is FAM 2, a 1948 Bristol L6B with Beadle C32R body

62 • BUS PRESERVATION AND RALLIES: THE EARLY YEARS TO 1980

Ex-Bristol 8335, a 1955 Bristol KSW6B carries a radiator badge 'SVOS' – Swindon Vintage Omnibus Society?

Nicely posed up for photography is ex-Southdown Guy Arab IV PUF 647. This had also been at the 1973 rally when in the colours of Confidence, Oadby (see p. 32)

SHOWBUS RALLY – UXBRIDGE: 26–27 JUNE 1976

The 1976 event was known as the National Showbus Rally, the 'National' recognising sponsorship from National Travel.

Two vehicles that had travelled down from Birmingham to attend Showbus were ex-Birmingham 1107 (CVP 207) 1937 Daimler COG5/Metro-Cammell and 1486 (GOE 486) 1947 Daimler CVA6/Metro-Cammell.

From the Leicester Museum of Technology came Leicester 164, a 1958 Leyland PD3/1 with Willowbrook H41/33R bodywork.

Former Red & White C350, a 1950 Leyland PS1/1 fitted with a Lydney thirty-three seat coach body

For many years the Northampton fleet comprised entirely of Daimlers and this is a 1947 Daimler CVG6 with Northern Coachbuilders H30/26R bodywork. This was still owned by Northampton and had recently been restored to original livery for publicity purposes having previously been used as a trainer.

NATIONAL TRAMWAY MUSEUM, CRICH: 28 AUGUST 1976

The private preservation of trams predates that of buses; Southampton tram No. 45 became the first to be privately preserved upon withdrawal in 1948. After some years in storage, it was first on public display at the Montagu Motor Museum, Beaulieu from 1958-60 before moving to Crich in 1960. The Tramway Museum Society was formed in 1955. They acquired the site at Crich, Derbyshire in 1959 with the intention of creating a National Tramway Museum with a working tramway for horse, steam, and electric operation. Horse trams first ran in 1963 and visitors were first able to ride on an electric tram from July 1964. In 1968 came the first annual Grand Transport Extravaganza weekend at which all sorts of vehicles visit. The museum has now been renamed the Crich Tramway Village.

The August Bank Holiday Extravaganza at Crich Tramway Museum saw visiting preserved vehicles, traction engines, etc. On a visit in 1976 this former Blackpool bus was on display. EFV 300 is a 1951 Leyland PD2/5 with Burlingham full-fronted centre-entrance bodywork to Blackpool specification.

Two other buses at Crich. KBP 993, a 1948 Bedford OB/Duple ex-Silver Queen, Worthing, and NTB 403, a 1950 Guy Otter with Alexander body. This was originally a demonstrator before being sold to Hulleys, Baslow. Neither vehicle now exists – the Guy was reported as scrapped in 1984.

VICTORIA AND ALBERT MUSEUM: 1976

RT1702 was one of four buses that inaugurated the Circular Tour of London during the Festival of Britain in 1951. It later passed into preservation. In 1976 it was posed outside the Victoria & Albert Museum, which was holding a twenty-five year commemorative exhibition on the Festival of Britain. RT1702 was to feature again in 2000 as an exhibit at the Millennium Dome exhibition.

COBHAM BUS MUSEUM: 3 APRIL 1977

The London Bus Preservation Group had been founded by eleven preservationists in 1966. They drew up a set of six aims including 'To bring together for their mutual benefit all known owners of ex-London Transport vehicles where the object of ownership is the preservation of the vehicle for historical purposes'. At this stage there was no mention of acquiring premises to house vehicles or of creating a museum. The members' vehicles were housed in various locations, including rented barns and open-air storage at station car parks. Members' vehicles made regular appearances on the HCVC London-Brighton Run, while from 1970 the LBPG started organising the Bus of Yesteryear rallies.

The building that housed the Cobham Bus Museum in Redhill Road was acquired by the London Bus Preservation Group in 1972. Originally known as Depot 45, it was the surviving example of three similar buildings constructed by Vickers in the Second World War as out-stations to their main factory in Brooklands Road, Weybridge. During the war, it was used for constructing wing sections of Wellington bombers and for experimental work on a British equivalent to the German V2 rocket. After closure in 1958, it had various temporary leases until it was bought by the Group.

A first public opening took place in January 1973, attracting some 200 visitors. However, the first 'Open Day' was held on 6 April 1974, a Sunday chosen as it did not clash with any other events in the rally calendar. Two buses provided a half-hourly link to Weybridge Station where rail connections and public parking were available. Another bus connected with the hourly Green Line route 715 at Cobham. Some 400 people attended and contributed to museum funds through the admission price.

Open Days took place in the following years. Some visiting buses came, and these were parked either in Redhill Road or at Weybridge Station. When the car park there was full, the bus route was extended to the car park in Weybridge town centre. Only fully-licensed vehicles driven by qualified drivers were used on the connecting bus link services.

In 2006 the LBPG became a Trust, and eventually in 2011 the LBPT opened the magnificent new London Bus Museum at Brooklands.

The first Cobham Open Day was in April 1974, but I did not visit until 1977. Here standing at Weybridge station on the bus link to the museum is RT1320 (KLB 569) of 1950 with Saunders roof box body.

68 • BUS PRESERVATION AND RALLIES: THE EARLY YEARS TO 1980

Outside the museum site, passengers wait to board GS34 which was bought by an LBPG member in 1976. This was donated to the museum in 1999. It was later housed off-site for many years but reappeared in 2019 with the display of rarities and unrestored buses held there in June. In 2021, the display hall at the London Bus Museum was reorganised and GS34 became one of the exhibits on display.

HCVC LONDON TO BRIGHTON RUN: 1 MAY 1977

By now the HCVC London-Brighton run was an established annual event, although now without sponsorship. By 1977, the HCVC had grown to around 1,600 members owning between them around 3,000 vehicles.

Right: HCVC London – Brighton programme 1977

Below: Making its first Brighton appearance in 1977 was T31, the 1929 AEC Regal with LGOC body which was the last ex-LGOC bus to work for London Transport and the first London bus to be privately preserved. Bought in 1956 for £45, by now this was owned by Norman Anscombe and had been rebuilt from front entrance to its original rear entrance style between 1974 and 1977 and also refitted from diesel to petrol engine. Today this forms part of the London Bus Preservation Trust collection.

One bus that was making a repeat visit was TF 818, a 1930 Roe bodied Leyland Lion LT1 new to Lancashire United and later passing to Jersey in 1946. Withdrawn in 1958 it then passed to the Lincolnshire Vintage Vehicle Society in 1959. The LVVS was founded in 1959 and have been regular supporters of the Run. TF 818 was first entered in 1967.

Interestingly this bus was not listed in the programme, so may have been a substitute for another entrant. CAP 211 was a 1940 Bristol K5G with ECW bodywork, converted to open-top seaside work by its owners Brighton Hove & District. It later passed to Thames Valley for an inland open-top service through the Thameside countryside. In 2015 it was listed as having been exported to Europe.

SOUTHEND RALLY: 5 JUNE 1977

By now into its fourth year, Southend attracted a total of 112 participants, although only one of these was of pre-war vintage.

A long way from its original working area, former Red & White S1449 is a 1949 Leyland PS1/1 with Lydney B35F body. It was new to Griffin, Brynmawr.

Much more local in origin is EJN 638, a 1953 Bristol LS6G/ECW C39F which started life with Westcliff-on-Sea Motor Services before being absorbed into Eastern National.

Entered by Delaine, Bourne was their No. 48 (OCT 566), a 1959 Leyland PD3/1. It carries bodywork by Yeates of Loughborough – one of only two double-deck vehicles to be bodied by this company. In 2018 this was listed as being resident in Holland. The other Yeates bodied double-decker, Delaine 50 (RCT 3) has been retained by the company as part of their Heritage Trust, and Delaine have continued to be regular supporters of bus rallies as well as opening a museum building.

SOUTHSEA RALLY: 12 JUNE 1977

This was organised by the Vintage Transport Association, once again held on the Common and attracting 106 entrants.

Former West Monmouthshire 9 (SAX 186), a 1957 Leyland Titan PD2/40 fitted with Willowbrook lowbridge bodywork. In 2018 this vehicle was listed by the PSV Circle as exported to Japan.

Another of the vehicles retained by Portsmouth Corporation. RV 3412 is a 1933 Leyland TD2 with English Electric body that became towing lorry TW2. They also kept TW1 (RV 3411) converted to a tower wagon.

SHOWBUS RALLY – UXBRIDGE: 25–26 JUNE 1977

As 1977 was the year of HM the Queen's Silver Jubilee, the rally was renamed the National Showbus Jubilee Rally. A total of 139 entrants participated.

1977 saw the repatriation of London Q1 trolleybus 1812 from Santandar-Astillero in Spain. Destined for the British Trolleybus Society at Sandtoft and eventual rebuild to London condition, it was exhibited at Uxbridge in 'as acquired' condition with offside entrances, etc. Alongside is TXV 909, a former London Transport AEC Mercury tower wagon, 1076Q, now with Reading Transport. This had towed the trolleybus to the rally.

This was not the only trolleybus at Uxbridge, for also entered was Hastings & District 3, a Dodson bodied Guy open-topper from the original fleet of 1928. In 1953, coronation Year, it was decorated and illuminated and then spent each summer running along the seafront between St. Leonards and the Fishmarket in this form. Hastings trolleybuses closed down in 1959, but the Guy was fitted with a diesel engine so that it could continue to run in service. Still owned by Hastings Borough Council, this then made appearances at several local rallies and events.

Oxford 16, a 1932 AEC Regent with Brush open-top body, is nowadays normally a static exhibit in the Oxford Bus Museum but was being rallied in 1977. Conversion to open-top was effected by subsequent owner Gosport & Fareham (Provincial). Note the board celebrating the Silver Jubilee.

BOURNEMOUTH OPEN DAY: 24 JULY 1977

1977 marked the seventy-fifth anniversary of Bournemouth Corporation Transport, and to celebrate this an Open Day was held at the Mallard Road garage on 24 July. A representative selection of past and present vehicles was on display.

In this line up, we see a Leyland PD2 and trolleybuses 202 (ALJ 986), 1935 Sunbeam MS2/Park Royal O40/29R and 212 (KLJ 346), 1950 BUT 9641T/Weymann H31/25D. Beyond these is a preserved 1954 Henschel from Baden-Baden, Germany and the ex-Huddersfield tower wagon VH 6217.

In 1962, Bournemouth took the last batch of trolleybuses bought in Britain. Nos. 295-303 were Sunbeam MF2Bs with Weymann dual-door, dual staircase bodies, the forward entrance being ahead of the front axle. They only lasted to April 1969 when the trolleybus network closed. Both 297 and 301 were on display. No. 299 is also preserved. I believe No. 297 was giving rides around the depot towing a generator trailer.

BRISTOL RALLY: 21 AUGUST 1977

The Bristol Rally and Avon Run held at Canons Marsh, Bristol started in 1975, organised by the Bristol Omnibus Preservation Society. 1977 was the first year I visited.

Above: A selection of the entrants can be seen in this view. The main subject is Midland Red 3750, a 1950 built BMMO S12 with Metro-Cammell B44F body. Midland Red built many of their own vehicles and were quick off the mark with this design of underfloor engine single-decker.

Opposite above: Seen before full repainting had taken place, NHY 947 is former Bristol 2815, a 1951 Bristol LWL6B with ECW full-front thirty-five seat coach bodywork. With the advent of underfloor engine coaches around this time, the front-engine chassis like this began to look old-fashioned so some bodybuilders opted for a full front design rather than the traditional half cab layout in an attempt to look more modern.

Opposite below: Preservation did not just extend to old British buses! This is a 1964 International Harvester with Superior (Ohio) B44F body that came from the United States Air Force. Originally registered 64B 2428 it had now received a modern British registration.

BRISTOL RALLY: 21 AUGUST 1977 • 77

NEWCASTLE: SUMMER 1977

For the summer of 1977, Tyne and Wear Transport ran a number of special events as part of the Queen's Silver Jubilee celebrations. A special service 44 ran from Central Station to Gosforth Park on weekdays from June 1 to September 24 using vintage buses that would have been in service when the Queen came to the throne. One of these was a former Newcastle 1948 Leyland PD2/1 with Leyland bodywork in the old blue livery. This had been withdrawn in 1969 and was owned by the County Council Museums Department. This later passed to the Northern Counties Bus Preservation Group. The other bus was a privately owned 1950 AEC Regent III with Northern Coachbuilders bodywork in the later yellow livery (see p. 93)

COBHAM BUS MUSEUM: 2 APRIL 1978

At the Museum on the service connecting it to Weybridge station is MLL 740. This is one of the 1953 AEC Regal IV vehicles with Park Royal bodies operated by London Transport on behalf of British European Airways to take passengers from the London air terminal to Heathrow Airport before there was any rail link.

The yard at the back of the museum was used to mount themed displays of vehicles. Here in 1978 we see a fascinating selection of prototypes. On the left is RM3, the 1957 Routemaster prototype fitted with a Leyland engine and originally numbered RML3. This was preserved by the London Bus Preservation Group and was later rebuilt with the original style of radiator fitted. In the middle is XTC 684, the 1955-built prototype Leyland Lowloader LFDD which would be the predecessor for the Atlantean. On the right was then almost new British Leyland B15 prototype BCK 706R which was tested by London Transport and led to orders for the Leyland Titan T class.

HCVC LONDON TO BRIGHTON RUN: 7 MAY 1978

The 1978 run was the first to be sponsored by truck makers Fodens Ltd. Extensive publicity drew large crowds both along the road and at Brighton but traffic congestion on the roads caused many late arrivals.

Above: Another of the many early Southdown buses that have survived. CD 5125 made its Run debut in 1977 and was back for 1978. A 1920 Leyland N, it was originally fitted with a charabanc body but was rebodied in 1928 by Short Bros. Sold in 1935, it was later converted into a house, complete with tiled roof. It was rescued and restored over a ten-year period. This retains the forward control layout of early buses but has the luxury of a windscreen and pneumatic tyres.

Opposite above: We saw AEC Regal III KYD 151 earlier in 1972 in as acquired state (see p. 27). Here it was in 1978, fully restored to the original owner's livery.

Opposite below: Making its first rally appearance at the 1978 and a class winner was HB 4060. A 1932 Bedford WLB with Davies twenty-seat bodywork, this had been owned by Williams, Blaina, but was found derelict in Leicestershire in 1974 and was bought and restored by a Mr Flynn.

HCVC LONDON TO BRIGHTON RUN: 7 MAY 1978 • 81

ENFIELD PAGEANT OF MOTORING: 28–29 MAY 1978

The first Enfield Pageant of Motoring was held at the Enfield Playing Fields in 1978 by the Enfield & District Veteran Vehicle Society which had been formed in 1961. The aim was to raise funds towards a future museum building (now the Whitewebbs Museum of Transport). The event was a huge success in terms of money made and all in excellent weather conditions; it attracted over 600 exhibitors This would go on to become an annual event.

Amongst the bus entrants were ex-London Transport GS17, at this time owned by Sampsons of Cheshunt, and preserved RT2553 (LYF 278) with Park Royal bodywork.

Also on display was this 1949 Bedford OB/Duple, ex-Kirbys of Bushey Heath. This coach later returned to active use as a heritage coach in the fleet of Alexcars, Cirencester.

SOUTHEND RALLY: 4 JUNE 1978

A unique vehicle in the Maidstone & District fleet was LC1 'The Knightrider'. Registered NKN 650, this was a 1951 Commer Avenger with a Harrington body seating only sixteen and with tables and a drinks cabinet – a very early form of executive coach. At this time, it was preserved by M&D but was sold into private hands in 1998.

84 • BUS PRESERVATION AND RALLIES: THE EARLY YEARS TO 1980

Vehicles from the 1960s were now passing into preservation and here we have a former Royal Blue Bristol RELH6G from 1967 with ECW C45F bodywork.

Of course bus rallies do not just attract preserved vehicles and there were some interesting older vehicles still operating commercially as well as brand new vehicles being entered at rallies. This 1956 AEC Reliance with Burlingham Seagull C41C body was in service with and entered by Lewingtons of Cranham. It had started out with Reliance, Newbury, but has not survived.

SOUTHSEA RALLY: 11 JUNE 1978

For 1978, the Southsea Spectacular (as the rally was entitled), also included an optional Solent City Run from Chandlers Ford to Portsmouth. Entries were up nearly fifty per cent on 1977 and included preserved cars and commercials as well as buses.

Portsmouth's first trolleybus, 201 (RV 4649), a 1934 AEC 661T with bodywork by English Electric, was retained for preservation. It saw a period of display at the Montagu Motor Museum at Beaulieu before returning to its home city. This was given an outing, towed on to the Common for the 1978 Southsea Rally. Like the Thornycroft bus, this now resides at the Milestones Museum in Basingstoke (see p. 61)

Many Bournemouth vehicles had been saved by the mid-1970s and this is 147 (YLJ 147), a 1959 Leyland PD3/1 with Weymann body. Like other Bournemouth double-deck buses and trolleybuses of the 1950s, it has dual entrance and dual staircases.

Not all the entrants were from the south coast, and here is former Lancashire United No. 21 (116 JTD), a 1959 Guy Arab IV with Northern Counties body – a type well-favoured by this fleet.

SHOWBUS RALLY – UXBRIDGE: 24–25 JUNE 1978

The rally, again forming part of the Hillingdon Show, was once again sponsored by National Travel. Over 170 vehicles were expected with 163 actually appearing. Most took part in the Sunday morning road run to Windsor and back. There was a specially sponsored pre-war collection, a new class for ex-London GS and RF buses and the results of the Pictorialist-National Bus Photographic Competition. Commentary was by John Parke, the Editor of *Buses* magazine. A particular problem experienced though was traffic congestion when entrants were leaving the field at the end of the day.

Built by Midland Red in 1965 for speeding along the M1 between London and Birmingham, 5656 (BHA 656C) is a 1965 BMMO CM6T with forty-six seat body. This was withdrawn in 1974 and preserved in Birmingham.

As usual for Showbus, many operators sent examples of their latest deliveries. Of particular interest was this Foden-NC bought experimentally by the West Midlands PTE. Foden were attempting to make a comeback in the bus market with this model, but it would be the locally produced MCW Metrobus, an example of which was also entered, that would find favour with the PTE into the 1980s.

WEYMOUTH RALLY: 2 JULY 1978

Another rally with an increasing number of entrants each year, this eighth occasion passing the 100 mark.

JVF 528 is a Bedford OB/Duple which was in the colours of Mulleys, Ixworth, Suffolk. These days this coach resides in the Oxford Bus Museum.

You go all the way from London to Weymouth and see a vehicle emanating from Liverpool! A267 (VKB 900) is a 1957 AEC Regent V with Metro-Cammell H33/29R body. When withdrawn in 1976 it was the last ex-Liverpool Corporation AEC in service with Merseyside PTE. This was entered by the Mersey & Calder Bus Preservation Group, earning them the award for the furthest-travelled entrant.

LANCASTER RALLY: 16 JULY 1978

While on a holiday tour in the north-west I took in a rally held at Lancaster, which produced a lot of locally based vehicles that never made it to my usual haunts in the south. The Lune Valley Run was from Morecambe to the Hornsea Pottery Leisure Park in Lancaster and was held to celebrate 75 years of Lancaster City Transport (which had absorbed Morecambe & Heysham in 1974). There was also a Lancaster Depot Open Day.

From the local Lancaster fleet, NTF 466, a 1952 Daimler CVG5 with Northern Counties body, had still been in passenger service in their current blue livery and lettered for the Queen's Silver Jubilee a year earlier. Now retired and restored to an earlier livery it would be placed on loan to the North West Museum of Transport.

Two Leylands from the Burnley Colne & Nelson fleet. 23 (HHG 23), a 1959 Tiger Cub PSUC1/1 and 45 (CHG 545), a 1954 PS2/14, both bodied by East Lancs. Note the board with rally plaques in front of the radiator of the PS2.

UHW 343 was a 1955 Albion Victor FT39AL with a Heaver 37 seat body bought new as a non-PSV bus by Glenside Hospital, Bristol. By 1992 it had passed into use by travellers in Cornwall as a mobile home. It suffered rear end damage and was consigned to a scrapyard. Rescued again, the new owner shortened the chassis and built a new cab. It was purchased by Mike Jefferies in 2011, then by Tesco's Supermarkets who had it rebuilt as a replica box van. As such it was entered in the 2015 London to Brighton Run.

A typical Lancashire product for a Lancashire operator. Rawtenstall 18 (RTC 822), a 1953 Leyland PD2/12 with East Lancashire bodywork.

SPU 985 is a rare Leyland Olympic HR44 from 1951 with Weymann DP40F body that ran for Jennings of Ashen. This was at this time with the Ribble Vehicle Preservation Group and kept at the former Steamport Railway Museum at Southport.

This little 1931 Dennis 30cwt with Short eighteen seat bodywork is now part of the FOKAB (Friends of King Alfred Buses) collection at Winchester. However, in 1978 it was with an owner from Liverpool, hence its appearance at Lancaster.

LONDON BUS RALLY, BROCKWELL PARK: 22–23 JULY 1978

The Lambeth Country Show is an event held annually in July at Brockwell Park. Until the 1980s this used to include traction engines and preserved vehicles but has since become more of a community cultural and music festival. In 1978, a London Bus rally and road run was added to this, sponsored by Grey-Green Travel. There were 100 vehicles entered, most of which attended. This would be repeated in 1979.

WAL 782 is not quite what it seems as it is a Barton rebuild. The chassis is a 1948 Leyland PS1 originally registered CWH 262. In 1957 Barton had it rebodied with this Willowbrook lowbridge double-deck body and re-registered. In 1978 it was with an owner from Fairseat, Kent. Now fully restored to Barton colours it is part of the Barton Cherished Vehicle Collection.

JJ 4379 was originally London Transport STL 162 until rebodied as breakdown tender 832J in 1950. The D.J. Slater publication *Preserved Buses, Trolleys & Trams* (1993 edition) reported this as 'Sold 1992 and later scrapped' but I am happy to say that this was incorrect, and JJ 4379 was fully restored when I saw it at Brooklands in October 2018.

NEWCASTLE: JULY 1978

Privately preserved Newcastle 341, a 1950 AEC Regent III with Northern Coachbuilders body, was returned to service in its home city on a Centenary Bus Service in 1978, having previously also worked on a Silver Jubilee route 44 in 1977. It was photographed near the central station.

SANDTOFT GATHERING: 30 JULY 1978

The origins of Sandtoft lie in the formation of the Reading Transport Society by Michael Dare in 1961 with the aim of preserving one of the town's pre-war trolleybuses, about to be replaced by new trolleybuses. 1939 AEC 661T No. 113 (ARD 676) was acquired in September 1961, becoming the UK's first privately preserved trolleybus, and was kept at the premises of a local coach operator, Smiths of Reading. Next year it was joined by London No. 260, which had also been privately purchased. Word got around, and soon South Shields No. 204 and Cardiff No. 203 had been presented to the Society, while Bournemouth No. 212 and Derby No. 172 were bought by the Society, along with a pre-war Reading AEC motorbus. The nucleus of a museum collection had been established. As most remaining trolleybus systems closed down during the 1960s, other groups and individuals began to acquire vehicles for preservation and the idea of creating a working museum began to emerge. In 1968, Michael Dare heard about four acres of land for sale at a disused ex-RAF airfield at Sandtoft in the area known as the Isle of Axholme in Lincolnshire. The Society did not have sufficient money themselves to buy and develop the site. They approached other groups to make an alliance, and as a result the Sandtoft Transport Centre Association was formed and registered as a charity. Michael's mother agreed to buy the land, put up a depot building and rent the site to the Association.

The first seven trolleybuses (and one Reading bus) moved on site in 1969 and were soon joined by others. The museum held its first open day in 1971 – the forerunner to the present annual Sandtoft Gathering. In that year the Reading Transport Society changed their name to the British Trolleybus Society to reflect their wider interest. A 14-vehicle extension building was built in 1972, and a second extension for 22 vehicles was added in 1973. By this time the last trolleybus system at Bradford had closed down and several Bradford vehicles joined the burgeoning collection.

1973 also saw another landmark for the growing museum, as it was in that year that trolleybuses were first able to operate under the wires. Overhead wiring had been commenced in 1971, and now electric power was provided from a diesel generator built on the back of a lorry. This worked satisfactorily and in fact it was not until the 1990s that mains electricity was used to power the wiring.

The original groups that formed the Sandtoft Transport Centre Association have gone their various ways since then, and the site is now run by the Sandtoft Transport Centre Ltd., a registered charity. The Trolleybus Museum at Sandtoft, to give it its official title, has continued to develop. It holds the world's largest collection of preserved trolleybuses, with some 45 resident vehicles both restored and awaiting restoration. These do not only comprise British vehicles, but include examples from Belgium, France, Germany and Portugal. There are also several motorbuses and a number of service vehicles, including four tower wagons to maintain the overhead wires.

There are regular open days, sometimes with themed events such as celebrating anniversaries, and the annual Sandtoft Gathering and the St. Leger Historic Vehicle Rally.

Another organisation, the National Trolleybus Association, was founded in November 1963 and continues to date. They are the owners of five trolleybuses, including Bournemouth No. 202, the world's only working open-top trolleybus. Before Sandtoft was established the NTA were proposing an alternative site near Ringwood, Hampshire but this idea lapsed as Sandtoft and the East Anglia Transport Museum at Carlton Colville gained wiring.

I did not visit the Centre until the 1978 Gathering and unfortunately the weather on that occasion was atrocious.

SANDTOFT GATHERING: 30 JULY 1978 • **95**

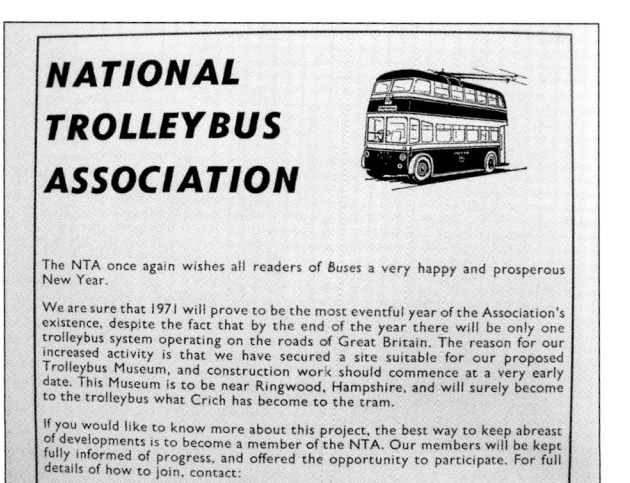

National Trolleybus Association advert from *Buses* magazine January 1971

A Sandtoft resident, Doncaster 94 was a 1947 Leyland PD2/1 that was rebodied in 1964 with the Roe body from a former trolleybus in the fleet.

Doncaster's trolleybuses ended in December 1963. One that was saved is 375 (CDT 636), a 1945 Karrier W with Roe body.

Some of the buses attending the Gathering. On the move is former Isle of Man Road Services 74 (KMN 504), an all-Leyland PD2 dating from 1949. At least, being a former airfield, there was hard standing for the vehicles.

BRISTOL RALLY: 20 AUGUST 1978

Former Western Welsh 13, a 1960 Harrington bodied Albion Nimbus. This is one of three of this batch that are listed as surviving in preservation.

LTX 311 is ex-Caerphilly and is a 1952 Leyland PS2 with Massey body. It had passed to Rhymney Valley when Caerphilly, Gelligaer and Bedwas & Machen had been merged in 1974, by then relegated to a towing vehicle. It was still in use as such at least until 1976.

As the blind states, this is a 1941 Bristol K5G, but with a long history. Bristol 8583 had started with Bristol as C3315 with covered top deck. It later passed to Brighton Hove & District where it became an open-topper. It then passed to Thomas Bros, Port Talbot as 'The Sandfields Belle'. It had now come back to Bristol for further service and was entered in the rally complete with National Bus Company symbol. It would later pass to Badgerline when Bristol was split up and received their livery. It was then used on loan by Guide Friday at Bath in their colours. Still owned by FirstGroup as successors to Badgerline it is now on loan to the Bristol Vintage Bus Group.

NATIONAL TRAMWAY MUSEUM, CRICH: 26–28 AUGUST 1978

At the Grand Transport Extravaganza there were some visiting buses parked over in the quarry area including Leeds 28, a 1948 Leyland PS1 with, of course, locally built Roe bodywork.

Giving rides around the site was this open back Paris Renault.

LONDON TRANSPORT COLLECTION, SYON PARK: 17 SEPTEMBER 1978

Syon Park had been home to the London Transport Museum since 1973 but the site was cramped, lacked expansion space and was too remote from the main tourist traffic. The solution to London Transport's problem came when the Covent Garden market moved to the site of the former BR steam depot at Nine Elms in 1974. The original Covent Garden became a conservation area. The old Flower Market, which is listed Grade II, was converted in 1978-9 to become the new London Transport Museum. This had been designed by William Rogers and built by William Cubitt & Co., opening in 1872. Syon Park closed at the end of 1978 to allow the exhibits to be moved to the new location once the site was prepared. To mark the closure, a Final Gala Day and Collector's Sale was held at Syon Park on Sunday 17 September 1978.

London Transport Collection, Syon Park leaflet 1978

London Transport Collection, Syon Park closure Gala Day poster

Announcing the London Transport Collection Final Gala Day and Collectors' Sale.

The London Transport Historic Vehicle Collection will close at the end of 1978 in preparation for its transfer to Covent Garden. The final special Gala Day and Collectors' Sale is to be held in the Thames Hall at Syon Park, Brentford on Sunday September 17.

ATTRACTIONS PLANNED

Hundreds of items of transport interest for sale including: Underground and bus equipment, signs and maps □ Breakdown vehicle displays □ Privately preserved buses and cars □ Working scale models □ Enthusiasts societies' stands □ Refreshments □ Passenger-carrying model railway.

Admission Normal prices: Your ticket for the London Transport Collection also gives admission to the Thames Hall (Adults 40p, Children 25p).
Times Thames Hall Market open 11 00 to 17 00. London Transport Collection open 10 00 to 18 00.
Underground—Hammersmith, then bus 267 or Gunnersbury then buses 237 or 267. Buses E1 and E2 run on 17 Sept. (and every Sunday) beyond Brentford to Syon Park. British Rail to Gunnersbury or Kew Bridge then buses 237 or 267.

Most other attractions at Syon Park—the Gardens and Gardening Centre, Great Conservatory, Aquarium and Aviary and World of Motoring will be open at their usual prices.

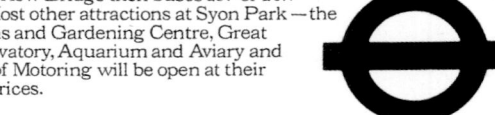

London General AEC K502 of 1920. This is not the example in the London Transport Museum collection (K424) but has been owned by Barry Weatherhead, Woburn Sands since the 1960s.

Also on display at Syon Park, trolleybus 260 from the London Trolleybus Preservation Society. As explained earlier, this had originally been selected for preservation by London Transport but was later rejected and then saved from the scrap man. Restored to running order, this later ran tours at Reading and Bournemouth before these systems closed, before finding a new home at the East Anglia Transport Museum.

PRESERVATION SITES AND VEHICLES IN THE LATE 1970s

In 1978 there was an open-air yard at Woolwich in south-east London, only a few minutes from the town centre where preserved buses and trolleybuses were being kept and worked on. The site was walled and gated, but the vehicles were exposed to the elements and potential theft and vandalism. In this view is LFJ 931, the ex-Greenslades 1951 Daimler CVD6 /Duple that had earlier been housed at the yard of Continental Pioneer in Richmond. Next to it is EAP 4 which was earlier seen at Hove. An ex-Walsall trolleybus is also in view.

Two of the other vehicles at Woolwich. CVH 741 is a 1947 Karrier MS2 trolleybus from Huddersfield with Park Royal body. Alongside is another of the former BEA Regal IVs, MLL 735, later used by London Transport as uniform issue unit 1468W. Both of these do still survive – the trolleybus with the National Trolleybus Association and MLL 735 with London Vintage Bus Hire, Northfleet.

PRESERVATION SITES AND VEHICLES IN THE LATE 1970s • **101**

Two more vehicles at Woolwich in June 1978. 780 JGY is former Jersey 27 (J 8588) 1959 Leyland PD2/31 with Reading bodywork which was fully restored. Awaiting attention is ex-London Transport GS55.

Noted stored and partially sheeted over in the old coach station at Cheltenham in July 1978 was this former Black & White Bristol L6G with Duple bodywork dating from 1948. In 2018 this was listed as being part of the Bristol Road Transport Collection but has since changed hands. I have not seen this since or a photo of it restored.

A coach that has been fully restored for some years is MMR 552, a 1955 Leyland Tiger Cub PSUC1/2 with Harrington C41C body new to Silver Star. In July 1978, I found it parked on the premises of Knubley, Bruton.

Some vehicles have survived into preservation because their former operators did not send them for scrap at the end of their working lives but just dumped them at the back of their yard. One such company was South Notts of Gotham, who would later be taken over by Nottingham City Transport. This veritable selection of antiques was on site in October 1979. They include 49 (MRR 339), a 1951 Leyland PD2/12 with Leyland body and 35 (JNN 97), a Leyland PS1/Duple. These did not survive, but the oldest vehicle (with the ladder propped up against it) No. 17 (VO 8846), a 1933 Leyland Lion LT5 with Willowbrook body is now safely under cover at the now Nottingham Hertitage Railway (formerly known as Great Central Railway (North).

Another company notorious for just dumping old vehicles was Berresford of Cheddleton, Staffs. Taken in 1978, this is former Stockport EDB 548, a 1951 Leyland PD2 with Leyland bodywork, stored in a building that hardly offered any protection from the weather. This did not survive, but similar EDB 562 is with the Museum of Transport, Manchester.

HCVC LONDON TO BRIGHTON RUN: 6 MAY 1979

Making its debut was DOD 518, a 1939 Bristol L5G ex-Western National No. 333. This has the pre-war style of high-mounted radiator but was rebodied in 1950 by Beadle of Dartford. Withdrawn in 1960, it had later served as a drivers' tea room.

Southdown converted a batch of 1938 Leyland TD5s to recovery vehicles and four of these survive. No. 0182 (EUF 182) was entered on the Run in 1979. Converted in 1957, it remained in service until 1971.

SOUTHAMPTON RALLY: 6–7 MAY 1979

A one-off rally was held on Southampton Common to celebrate the centenary of Southampton City Transport. A wide range of preserved and current vehicles attended, including vehicles from many of the other municipal and PTE fleets and even two modern buses from France (from Caen and Le Havre).

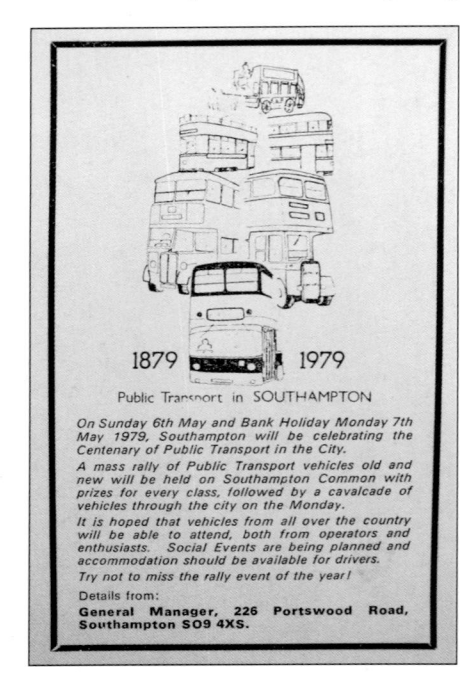

Above left: Southampton Rally advert

Above right: On Southampton Common is Exeter 43, the 1949 Daimler CVD6/Brush we saw in 1976 at the yard of Continental Pioneer, Richmond (see p. 54). Alongside is ex-London Transport RTL453, a regular attender of rallies which these days is owned by Ensignbus, Purfleet.

Left: Also on display was former Ribble 753 (FV 5737), a 1936 Leyland TS7 which was rebodied by Duple in 1950. This was another vehicle from the extensive collection of Mr Hoare of Chepstow.

WEST BROMWICH RALLY: 13 MAY 1979

A new event first held in May 1978 was the Sandwell Historic Vehicle Parade and Transport Show at Sandwell Park, West Bromwich.

At Sandwell Park in 1979 was this rare combination of a 1948 Maudsley Marathon II chassis with a body by Trans-United. It worked for Hackett, Manchester and is preserved by the Coventry Transport Museum. The Bedford OB alongside, SS 7376, was new to McKinley, Prestonpans in 1949. It later became owned as a heritage vehicle by East Yorkshire, but by 2021 the PSV Circle recorded it as having changed hands again.

106 • BUS PRESERVATION AND RALLIES: THE EARLY YEARS TO 1980

Vehicles from the various fleets that became the West Midlands PTE were on show and representing Wolverhampton is trolleybus 433 (DUK 833) a 1946 Sunbeam W/Roe. This is normally kept at the Black Country Living Museum at Dudley where it is able to run under the wiring installed there.

Single-deck buses made up only a small proportion of the Birmingham City Transport fleet, but four of this batch of 1950 Leyland PS2/1 buses have survived. Birmingham 2231 has a Weymann B34F body.

SOUTHEND RALLY: 3 JUNE 1979

Hants & Dorset 677 started out in 1950 as a Bristol LL6B with a Portsmouth Aviation half-cab coach body. However, in 1961 the company had it lengthened and rebodied by ECW with this full-frontal body for OMO bus work. The rear of these vehicles was tapered upwards to prevent them grounding when boarding the Sandbanks chain ferry on route 7 from Bournemouth to Swanage.

Now fully restored and repainted was the Eastern National Preservation Group's ex-Moores, Kelvedon 1963 Guy Arab IV with Massey bodywork 373 WPU. (see earlier p. 48)

SOUTHSEA RALLY: 10 JUNE 1979

Rather dull weather at Southsea and here is a coach a long way from its original stamping ground. BMS 405 is a 1948 Daimler CVD6SD with Burlingham C33F body, ex-Alexander D10. It passed to Alexander (Northern) as ND10 when the fleet was split. This is now with a preservationist back in Scotland.

Looking somewhat shabby as renovation was ongoing is former East Kent JG 8720, a 1937 Dennis Lancet II rebodied by Park Royal in 1949. A fresh coat of paint would soon work wonders…

SHOWBUS RALLY – UXBRIDGE: 23–24 JUNE 1979

The 1979 rally was entitled the Great British Showbus Rally and this time the Sunday road run was to the AEC works at Southall. Sponsorship this year was from Grey-Green Travel who also sponsored the London Bus rally at Brockwell Park. This was the last year that Showbus was held at Uxbridge, the traffic congestion problems at the end of the day prompting a move away. The 1980 Showbus would be held at Thorpe Park near Staines.

Showbus has always been about presenting the latest in bus and coach design as well as preserved vehicles, and the 1979 event gave visitors one of the first opportunities to travel on an articulated bus in Britain. While commonplace in Europe, such vehicles had not been permitted in the UK, but the South Yorkshire PTE were about to introduce a free service with them in Sheffield and this MAN demonstrator was used to provide a free connection from Uxbridge station as seen here. It had also been used the previous year at the Motor Show held at Birmingham NEC. Seen with a German registration plate, this would later become CLM 346T.

A line up of Reading buses past and present. From right to left are preserved No. 12 (PRD 32) 1959 AEC Reliance/Burlingham; No. 3 (MRD 146) 1957 AEC Regent III/Park Royal; and a then new MCW Metrobus.

Posed for photographs, a 1961 West Riding Guy Wulfrunian with Roe body. West Riding were the main takers of this generally unsuccessful design, although UCX 275 came to them from County Motors Lepton.

London Transport never had any of their eighty-four strong GS class in central area red livery. However, this did not deter the owners of preserved GS67 from creating a fascinating 'might-have been' by painting it in red.

WEYMOUTH RALLY: 1 JULY 1979

Taking part in the Weymouth rally on 1 July 1979 was the now preserved former Southern National's first Bristol LS 1701 of 1953. This vehicle now forms part of the Science Museum collection, housed at Wroughton airfield near Swindon.

An example of a preserved bus in a fictitious livery. We saw former Caerphilly LTX 311 at Bristol in 1978 in original colours (see p. 96). At Weymouth in 1979 it was entered painted in the colours of Jones, Aberbeeg.

A preserved bus in National Bus Company livery! London Country RT1018 dated from 1948 but survived in service long enough to gain NBC leaf green livery along with RT604. Both then passed into preservation.

LONDON BUS RALLY, BROCKWELL PARK: 21-22 JULY 1979

The second London Bus Rally was held at Brockwell Park in association with the Lambeth Country Show in 1979 and included a road run over London bridges. Again, there were also many traction engines and other commercial vehicles present besides the buses. However, this event was not advertised for 1980.

UFJ 292 is a former Exeter Corporation 1957 Guy Arab IV with Massey bodywork.

Entered by Potteries Motor Traction was this 1959 Leyland Atlantean with Weymann bodywork which had been painted in a 1932 style of livery to mark the centenary of public road transport in North Staffordshire. This vehicle has since been preserved.

BRISTOL RALLY: 19 AUGUST 1979

A Bristol Bristol in Bristol! C8322 is a late example of the KSW6B model, built in 1956 when the Lodekka had already succeeded this in most fleets' intake. The C prefix and coat of arms with the fleetname indicate that this was part of the Bristol city fleet rather than used on country services.

From the fleet of Neath & Cardiff, WWN 191 is a 1960 AEC Reliance with Harrington Cavalier coachwork. This company ran limited stop express services between Swansea and Cardiff until they were absorbed into National Welsh.

150 YEARS OF LONDON BUSES: 1979

In 1979 London Transport celebrated 150 years since George Shillibeer first introduced the omnibus to London in 1829. There were a series of events in which the vehicles saved by London Transport and its predecessor, the London General Omnibus Group would be paraded, alongside those preserved privately by the London Bus Preservation Trust and other organisations and private individuals. It would also mark the final service of two classic vehicle types from the 1950s – the RT and the RF. Both events were celebrated in style and many of the final vehicles in service would pass on into preservation.

Additionally, twelve Routemaster buses were painted in the livery of Shillibeer's original horse bus, as was also Fleetline DMS2646 (sponsored by British Leyland) and RCL2221 which had been converted to a cinema bus.

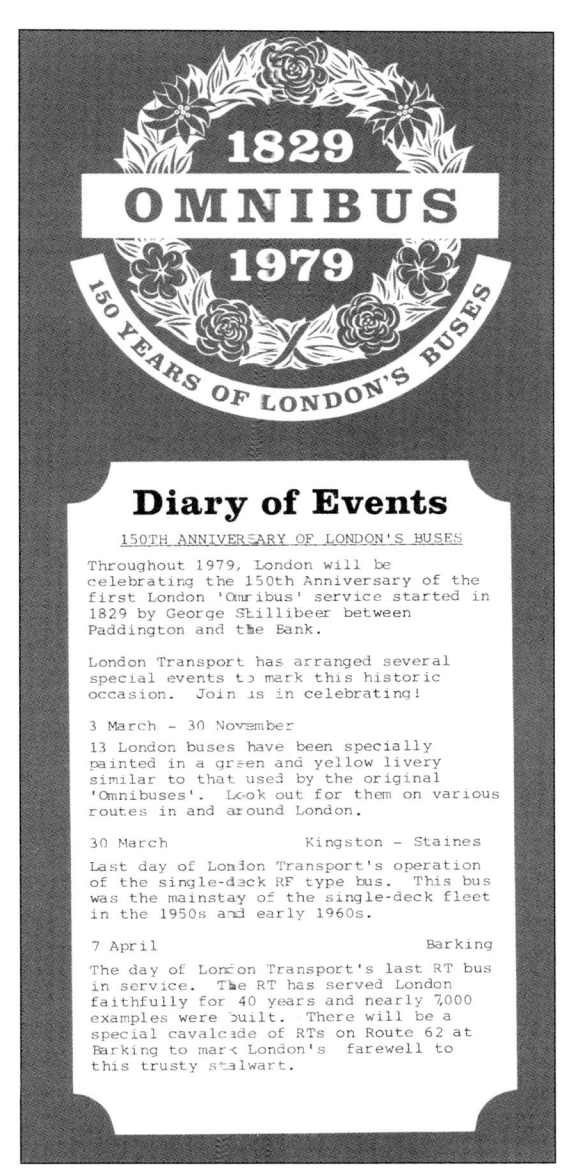

London Transport 1979 Diary of Events leaflet

London Transport 1979 Easter Bus Parade leaflet

116 • BUS PRESERVATION AND RALLIES: THE EARLY YEARS TO 1980

The first major event of the year was a rally and parade in Battersea Park on Easter Sunday, 15 April. Seen here is the London Bus Preservation Group's Dennis 3-ton D142 which had been restored in 1972. This had attended the first Brunelzeebub rally at Uxbridge in 1973.

Also at Battersea Park, it was fitting that the prototype RT1 should be on show, just a week after the last RTs had ended service on route 62 from Barking garage. This vehicle was nearly lost to UK preservation. It had remained with LT until 1978 when sold into preservation but was then exported to the USA. It was repatriated in the 1980s and later given a full restoration at a cost of over £200,000. Despite an offer from abroad it was finally acquired by the London Bus Museum in 2010 which had to raise the asking price of £150,000 within a year through an appeal fund.

Above left: London Transport 1979 Hyde Park Parade leaflet

Above right: The main event of the year was on Sunday 8 July, almost 150 years to the day since George Shillibeer had started his pioneer horse bus service. Several vehicles including the 1929 built replica of Shillibeer's horse bus ran over part of the original route from London Wall to Paddington before joining the main rally in Hyde Park, where it was seen. This was probably the first time the horse bus had run on the road since the 1929 centenary celebrations. It had most recently been an exhibit at the now closed London Bus Collection at Syon Park.

C111 is a 1936 Leyland Cub with Park Royal RC18F bodywork. There were eight of these unusual forward-control models with observation-style bodies which had extensive luggage space below the raised rear section. They were for a nightly 'Interstation' service between the main line termini when the Underground was closed and carried a non-standard blue and cream livery.

Innovation, 1960s style. With the authorization of one-person operated double-deckers in 1966, London Transport devised a front-entrance, rear-engined variant of the Routemaster. The hydraulic braking, power steering and about sixty per cent of the body parts came from the RM design. However, with a lack of sales of the Routemaster other than to Northern General and with competition from the Leyland Atlantean, Daimler Fleetline and Bristol VR, it was not considered commercially viable and FRM1 would remain unique. At least it has been retained by the London Transport Museum and is still sometimes rallied.

Above left: London Transport 1979 Horse bus service leaflet

Above right: Between 9 July and 30 September, passengers had the opportunity to ride on a horse bus from Baker Street and around the inside perimeter road of Regent's Park to London Zoo. Three horse buses were used and this a c. 1890 Andrews Star Omnibus Co. garden seat bus, a company in operation from 1892 to 1909.

COBHAM BUS MUSEUM: 13 APRIL 1980

After the 1979 Cobham Gathering, it was realised that bus parking space was becoming a serious problem. An approach to British Aerospace led to the Sandpits car park site opposite their headquarters being made available in 1980. This was conveniently located halfway between the Museum and Weybridge station. Nearly sixty visiting vehicles attended and were accommodated there.

The event continued to grow in popularity, attracting more visitors and more visiting vehicles. This increase caused congestion problems and delays as buses struggled to unload passengers and turn at the museum. This would lead to a number of different sites being used in the 1980s and thereafter, especially after the British Aerospace factory closed. Indeed, it was not until the museum moved to a new purpose-built site at Brooklands in 2011 that a regular location for the Open Days could be established.

Seen outside the Museum on the connecting service from Weybridge is RMC4, the prototype Green Line Routemaster coach. This had passed to London Country Bus Services when London Transport was split up in 1970. Eventually this would pass into preservation, as have all the other prototype and pre-production Routemasters.

Taken at the Weybridge BAC Works was former London Transport RW2, one of three experimental AEC Reliances with Willowbrook B42D bodies bought in 1960. They all soon passed to Chesterfield Corporation, and after withdrawal from there, both RW2 and RW3 were later bought for preservation.

Former London Transport RF332 was acquired by the Cobham Bus Museum and converted as a towing vehicle.

HCVC LONDON TO BRIGHTON RUN: 4 MAY 1980

1980 was the third year with sponsorship by Foden. Among the participants was MTU 296, a 1948 Foden PVFE6 model from the local company Coppenhall of Sandbach, Cheshire, where Fodens were made. The bodywork is by Metalcraft.

A regular feature at Brighton, including the first Run in 1962, has been the Maxwell 1922 14-seat charabanc CJ 5052 owned by the National Motor Museum, Beaulieu, Hants. Lord Montagu of Beaulieu was a founder of the HCVC and later its president.

The Brighton Run started from Battersea Park. In this year there was a 'Wheels of Yesterday' rally held in Battersea Park on the following day, Bank Holiday Monday. Some of the Run participants remained for this but there were also other separate entrants including this former Swiss postbus, a 1948 Saurer.

EAST ANGLIA TRANSPORT MUSEUM, CARLTON COLVILLE: 15 JULY 1980

This museum was founded in 1965 when a group of local enthusiasts who had bought the body of Lowestoft tram No. 14 in 1962 decided to develop a museum in which to run it. The land was donated by Mr Bird, the founder and first chairman of the society. An early link was forged with the London Trolleybus Preservation Society, owners of London No. 260 at Reading. As a result, the Museum installed wiring for both trams and trolleybuses to run around the site. A notable first was achieved in January 1971 when London No. 1521 became the first preserved trolleybus to run under wires at a museum in Britain – two years ahead of Sandtoft. The museum first opened to the public on 28 May 1972, but regular trolleybus operation had to wait until May 1981 when a suitable road surface had been laid.

The link with London has continued to remain strong. The museum is home to three London trolleybuses, Nos. 260, 1201 and 1521 (which was the last to run in service). There is also a London tram, thus Carlton Colville is the only place where London trams and trolleybuses can be seen operating together. The London trolleybuses tend to be run on special events days and Bank Holidays. Visiting vehicles over the years have included 'Diddler' No. 1 and Q1 No.1768 from the London Transport Museum. The museum also has various other British and European trams and trolleybuses as residents, as well as buses and other commercial vehicles.

I did not visit Carlton Colville until 1980, so these pictures are from then.

Representing the former local Lowestoft fleet is 21 (GBJ 192), a 1947 AEC Regent II with locally-built ECW bodywork before it was restricted to state-owned fleets.

Ex-Eastern Counties X39 (ENG 707), a 1940 Bristol L5G converted to a towing lorry and Cardiff trolleybus 203 (CKG 193), 1942 AEC 664T/Northern Counties H38/32R await their turn for restoration.

Some repanelling work has been taking place on KW1961, a 1927 Leyland Lion PLSC3 new to Blythe & Berwick, Bradford. This had originally been repatriated from Jersey by Ken Blacker in 1959.

LINCOLNSHIRE VINTAGE VEHICLE SOCIETY

One of the early societies was the Lincolnshire Vintage Vehicle Society, founded in April 1959. Their first vehicle was a former Lincoln Corporation Leyland Lion which was donated to them and two other pre-war Leylands were bought from Jersey. At first the vehicles were kept in the Corporation bus garage and a former army premises, but a permanent site was located at Whisby Road just outside the city boundary. In the early years of preservation there was some official suspicion of such strange activity and the LVVS were told that they could not use the Lincoln coat-of-arms on their vehicles, so for a few years they used their own emblem. In 1966 a former army building was bought and re-erected at the Whisby Road site, and the LVVS first exhibited vehicles at the Lincolnshire Agricultural Show. A first annual Open Day at the Whisby Road museum site took place in 1969. Later the building was extended and by the 1980s it was open each Sunday from May to September. The collection is not just buses but includes other road vehicles, many with local connections. I first visited in 1982.

The first bus preserved by the LVVS in 1959 was VL 1263, a 1929 Leyland Lion LT1 with Applewhite B33R bodywork. After withdrawal in 1949 this had been transferred to the City Engineer's Department for use as a snowplough. This was photographed taking part in the 1986 London-Brighton Run after it had been completely rebuilt between 1984-6.

A vehicle that was entered at the first HCVC rally at Leyland back in 1958 was WH 1553, a 1929 Leyland Titan TD1 with outside staircase body, ex-Bolton No. 54. At the time this was owned by Leyland Motors who had planned to restore it, but in 1965 it was donated to the LVVS where it has remained since. Full restoration was completed in time for the 1970 London-Brighton Run.

An unusual vehicle from the Lincolnshire fleet taken at the museum site was LTA 752, a 1950 Bedford OB/Duple originally with Western National. This had been rebuilt with detachable side panels to allow it to run open-sided on Skegness seafront services. 2094 has since become part of the heritage fleet of Lodge's Coaches, High Easter, Essex.

LONDON TRANSPORT MUSEUM, COVENT GARDEN: 1980

The new museum was opened by Princess Anne on 28 March 1980. Ideally situated in the heart of a tourist area in Central London, this has been the home of the London Transport Museum ever since. A makeover in 1993 saw the insertion of a mezzanine floor to increase the exhibition space available. A further refit between 2005-07 has enabled the museum to take on the wider role of the various aspects of public transport under the TfL remit. The Covent Garden site is supplemented by the Museum Depot at Acton which holds the reserve collection. This opened in October 1999 and is publicly open on selected weekends and for pre-booked tours.

Presumably, when the Museum of British Transport at Clapham closed, this was regarded as too large a site to be retained for a purely London Transport Museum collection. With hindsight we could say that had this happened, the museum might have been big enough to house all the present collection at Covent Garden plus the reserve collection at Acton. The ancestry of the building as a garage would have added to the atmosphere, and there would have been easy access in and out for working exhibits to attend rallies. Maybe it could have had a gallery viewing a restoration area, as is the case at the National Railway Museum. But such concepts were unknown in 1973. Also, Clapham would not have been accessible to the Underground network to move railway exhibits in and out. However, most significantly Clapham was still not best placed for the crucial passing tourist traffic, particularly vital to the commercial sales at the museum shop. In this respect, Covent Garden has proved the ideal location and will continue to do so, backed up by the Museum Depot.

When Covent Garden first opened, vintage bus route 100 ran hourly from Covent Garden to Oxford Circus using either ST922 or the open-top Dennis D142. This lasted until 1983.

A view inside the new London Transport Museum at Covent Garden in May 1980 with Q55 and an RF behind. On the left can be seen 'Diddler' trolleybus No. 1 with its central single headlight, a vehicle preserved by London Transport in the continuing tradition set by the LGOC in the 1920s.

POSTSCRIPT

By 1980, events like the Cobham Gathering, Southend, Southsea and Bristol rallies, to name but a few, were now established alongside longer-running events such as the London to Brighton and Trans-Pennine Runs of the HCVC. Showbus had become the largest rally, a reputation it still holds, but had moved away from Uxbridge due to traffic congestion and would have several different locations in future years. Several transport museums had opened around the country. The London Transport Museum had found its permanent home at Covent Garden. Some bus companies were now celebrating their centenaries – Royal Blue and Ipswich Borough Transport would celebrate theirs with rallies in 1980; and in London 150 years had been celebrated in 1979. The number of vehicles being preserved had grown to such an extent that a first book to list all known vehicles *Preserved Buses* by Keith A. Jenkinson, the Hon. Registrar of the HCVC, published in 1976, had progressed to a second edition (1978) listing over 1,550 vehicles of some 270 different models. The preservation movement had grown into maturity and here seems a fitting point to end this story.

The 'Running Day' where preserved buses carry passengers over their former routes was not yet a feature before 1980 and the first such event in the former London Transport area would be at Amersham in 1988. However, an early foretaste of the future came on 19 April 1981 when two preserved London Transport RLH buses ran a tour over the old route 178 Maryland Station-Clapton Pond. This had been the last London route to use the type when they were withdrawn ten years earlier on 16 April 1971. Here the pair, RLH 23 in red and RLH 29 in green pose at Clapton Pond.

BIBLIOGRAPHY

CHRISTIE, David — *The London to Brighton Commercial Vehicles Run 1968 to 1987* (Stroud: Amberley, 2018)
ISLES, Martin — *The World's biggest bus rally: The history of Showbus* (in *Buses Focus* No. 8, Autumn 1997)
JENKINSON, Keith A. — *Preserved Buses* 2nd edition (Shepperton: Ian Allan, 1978)
JENKINSON, Keith A. — *Saved for posterity: Bus and coach preservation* (Stroud: Amberley, 2018)
KAYE, David — *Buses and trolleybuses 1919 to 1945* (London, Blandford, 1970)
MOON, George — *London Transport 260* (in *Preserved Bus* No. 21, January 2001)
PEART, Tony — *How it all began: The early days of bus rallies* (in *Buses Focus* No. 8, Autumn 1997)
SMITH, Graham — *London Buses A living heritage: Fifty years of the London Bus Museum* (Kettering, Silver Link, 2017)
SIMMONS, Jack — *Transport Museums of Western Europe* First published by George Allen & Unwin, 1970

Buses (bi-monthly / monthly magazine) (Hampton Court, Ian Allan, 1949 onwards, now Key Publishing)
Bus & Coach Preservation (monthly magazine) (Portsmouth, Presbus Publishing, 1998 onwards, now Meteor Books)
Preserved buses, trolleys & trams (2nd edition) (Birmingham, 1993)
Preserved buses (2021 edition) (London, The PSV Circle, 2021) and earlier editions
Most of the information about the HCVC/HCVS and the Brighton Run entrants has come from the excellent and comprehensive programmes produced for the event each year.